I0145478

Discipline Is Freedom

Discipline Is Freedom

Norm Sawyer

© 2024 Norm Sawyer
ISBN 10: 1-988226-66-X
ISBN 13: 978-1-988226-66-8
All rights reserved.

Cover Art: Kane Sawyer
Cover Graphics: Masud Choudhury

Published by

First Page Publishing
Kelowna, BC, Canada

Dedication

To all who have paid the price of becoming disciplined in the areas of their life's most difficult challenges. To those who have gone the extra mile to be sure that their objective was doing what was right, and doing it right.

Contents

Foreword

Because of the Lord's generous blessing, I have in my life a very dear friend and brother in Norm Sawyer. Norm has shared many valuable lessons with me over the years and offered me several opportunities through writing and publishing in order to grow in my faith and my craft. The Lord works in ways we may never understand and blesses us beyond our comprehension sometimes. Norm is one of those incomprehensible blessings to me, and as I've expressed to him, "'Blessing' isn't a big enough word to describe your friendship. Thank you for being in my life." Norm is always helping someone accomplish something, whether it is a spiritual or physical goal, or simply being a consistent, present genuine friend.

Norm is the most disciplined person I know, and the most dedicated and strongest 70-something I've ever seen in a workout video! By looking at him, no one would ever guess how difficult his path has been to get to where he is today. He is one of those people who doesn't just "inspire" me, he has actually affected changes in me – the way I think, study, write, see myself, interact with others, and the way I have grown in my faith. His life example is habit and life-changing because he doesn't just talk the talk. Norm has walked out every single part of his talk, and his life represents exactly who that is without saying another word. He puts in the real work, not just for himself but for anyone he's helping.

This book is full of help, and it was created with others in mind, just like everything else he does. In this book, Norm provides scriptural guidance throughout his life experiences in order to share how he exercised personal discipline to overcome—from childhood trauma all the way to his stroke, troubling after-effects, and subsequent diagnosis of Afib. Norm shares his incredible weight loss, health and fitness journey, fiscal responsibilities, and shares wisdom along the way to encourage us to apply the practice of discipline to lead a full, productive, meaningful life.

I've had the honor of sharing in the editing of several of Norm's books, and when I work on one of his books, I seem to get healing or solutions in an area in which I'm struggling. His wisdom always holds true, as I always find the Lord leading me into peace as I work on one of his projects. If it's truth and a life changed for the better that you are seeking, you are in the right place. I hope that you will find something helpful here for your own healing journey.

Jami Rogers, Coleman, Michigan
Co-author, Thoughts From A Friend

Introduction

Is God disciplined? I believe that He is intensely disciplined and we can agree that it takes an omniscient discipline to keep this universe moving as God intends it to move. We were created in His image and the transfer of His eternal breath was given to us at creation. Since it is God's breath keeping us alive, we also can become disciplined if we practice the art of being disciplined.

Philippians 3:12: **Not that I have already reached the goal or am already perfect, but I make every effort to take hold of it because I also have been taken hold of by Christ Jesus. I have not reached the perfection of what discipline offers, or what discipline is doing for me.** I am growing in discipline while adding its attributes to my character. I hope to become the version of who God made and wants me to be.

Disciplined people are not special, they are people who failed many times in the different endeavours of life but kept getting up until the failures became less frequent. Disciplined people are those who finally, after many attempts, have learned to recognize the signs and warnings of failure. They have learned to obey the instructions of doing what needs to be done to accomplish the task at hand. Discipline is the practice of avoiding the sin of complacency which is the default setting of the lazy. Disciplined people have fought their giants over and over again until the giants were defeated and bound with the same chains they used to keep the undisciplined ineffective. Discipline is freedom when lived within the strength of our heart's abilities.

Discipline is a gift from God. The more of God's anointed discipline we participate in, the more God reveals the eternal benefits of it. It's like a heavenly sweetener. The more we consume and submit to it, the more we crave the freedom it gives us.

Discipline is freedom.

This book is a testimony of my journey from sickness to health and weakness to strength in the different areas of my life. By applying discipline to my resolve and choices, I have found a way to be free as I became obedient to what discipline could offer, which offered a lot. For this, I am grateful to God for directing me in the direction of one who is disciplined in heart.

You Can't Steal My Discipline

Matthew 6:20 But store up for yourselves treasures in heaven, where moth and rust do not destroy, and where thieves do not break in and steal.

You cannot steal anyone's discipline that has become accustomed to the stabilizing rules of conduct, faithful results, and motivational strength that it gives those who are committed to being disciplined. What an amazing treasure this art is for those who have found and applied it to their lives. The reason I call it a treasure is that discipline is priceless if you use it to guide your life toward the calling God has placed upon your heart and the goals you have set. Without discipline, most ventures run off the rails and everything comes to a crashing halt including all the self-made promises of losing weight, studying more, working harder, breaking the addiction and the many other empty promises that flow from non-committed and undisciplined people.

Why do those who are committed to being disciplined in a craft, specialty, or training grow and develop better results in many areas of their lives? The Scriptures say that those who listen and apply the Lord's teachings will receive more understanding and the ability to walk in what is understood. Mark 4:25 **To those who listen to my teaching, more understanding will be given. But for those who are not listening, even what little understanding they have will be taken away from them.** Those who do not listen to the lessons of discipline will lose the strength of will they have left. They will also be easy targets to be robbed of whatever resolve they had left to fight the temptations of life, leaving them vulnerable to the attack of the enemy.

I have said, "Discipline is a cruel master, but a necessary companion to make a stand in life." Yes, there are times when discipline makes a demand on the will of our soul that seems so difficult at the time to follow through on the challenge, but when we obey and come through, there is victory. I try to hang out with those who have adopted the skills of this attribute so that I am encouraged to stay the course. Ask anyone who slipped away and gradually found themselves in a mess of their own making. It did not take much laziness for them to become indifferent and apathetic toward everyday challenges. Prov. 24:33 **Go ahead and take your nap; go ahead and sleep. Fold your hands and rest awhile, 34 but while you are asleep, poverty will attack you like an armed robber.**

The Apostle Paul could never have gone through what he suffered had he not been a man who was disciplined in his calling and anointing to minister the Word of God. How was he able to endure so much persecution and hardships, yet stay faithful to the Lord? 2Cor. 11:24 **Five times I** received from the Jews the forty lashes minus one. 25 **Three times I was beaten with rods, once I was stoned, three times I was shipwrecked. I have passed a night and a day in the deep sea;** 26 **In my frequent journeys, I have been in danger from rivers and from bandits, in danger from my countrymen and from the Gentiles, in danger in the city and in the country, in danger on the sea and among false brothers,** 27 **in labor and toil and often without sleep, in hunger and thirst and often without food, in cold and exposure.**

I know I am being sarcastic, but sheesh, a bit of discipline on our part would bring some resolve to our hearts. Today, we have people threatening to leave the faith because they have to park their cars so far from the front doors of the church, or the pastor didn't acknowledge and thank them because they brought toothpicks to the annual church picnic. We need to grow up in the maturity God is leading us in. Paul kept his emotions and body under control so that he would not become complacent or entitled in the ministry God had called him to. 1Cor. 9:27 **But I discipline my body and keep it under control, lest after preaching to others I myself should be disqualified.** No one could have stolen Paul's discipline, not even Satan.

Only Joshua and Caleb maintained their discipline of faith by believing the promises of God that the land of Canaan was given to the nation of Israel. In the mounting unbelief that the ten spies had created through a negative report, Caleb spoke boldly. Num. 14:9 **Only do not rebel against the LORD. And do not be afraid of the people of the land, because we will devour them. Their protection is gone, but the LORD is with us. Do not be afraid of them.** The sad thing was that the nation of Israel was on the doorstep of receiving God's promise but was not able to attain it because of a majority vote from a fickle and undisciplined people who believed the fears of the ten spies. Joshua and Caleb needed to maintain their discipline of faith toward God for another forty years till the promise was fulfilled. These men of faith were able to enter the land of Canaan because their discipline could not be stolen from them.

As I grow in the faith that Jesus Christ my Lord has established in my heart through His sacrifice on the cross, I will do my best to remain a faithful son of the Most High God. By grace, I will be disciplined in all areas of my life so that I may say as the Apostle Paul did at the end of his tour of duty on this earth. 2Tim. 4:7 **I have fought the good fight, I have finished the race, I have kept the faith.** I too want to be able to say to the enemy of my soul, "Through the mercy and grace of my Lord and Saviour Jesus, you cannot steal the discipline that I have in Christ! I have been paid for in full by the blood of Jesus. It is said it is done." Amen and amen!

Part One
Discipline Of Grace

True grace teaches us to abstain from sin and anything that leads to ungodly iniquity. The Word says that grace teaches us to say no or reject sinfulness and we do this while we wait for the glorious coming of our Lord Jesus. As the Word says, grace has been offered to all man and those who accept its saving power will walk fully in the blessing that grace provides. Titus 2:11 **For the grace of God has appeared that offers salvation to all people. 12 It teaches us to say "No" to ungodliness and worldly passions, and to live self-controlled, upright and godly lives in this present age, 13 while we wait for the blessed hope—the appearing of the glory of our great God and Savior, Jesus Christ**.

The arguments between believers in Christ concerning the abuse of grace have made me wonder. Some of the ministers say the extreme grace being taught, allows sin to be acceptable, and this is just unacceptable to them. They claim that this teaching is too loose and it permits people to think they are getting away with sin. Let me assure you, no one gets away with sin, whether they think it or not. Rom. 6:23 **For the wages of sin is death; but the gift of God is eternal life through Jesus Christ our Lord**. I do not believe grace is as fragile and delicate as their arguments state. We can be disciplined in grace like any other activity in life. Grace is holy because it comes from the heart of God, but not fracturable. The Lord's grace is not some weak ready-to-topple-over gift that might or might not work because of our shortcomings. John 1:16 **And of his fullness have all we received, and grace for grace.** 17 **For the law was given by Moses, but grace and truth came by Jesus Christ**. Grace is far stronger than people realize.

We sometimes forget that God, by His

grace, loved us first before we could do anything considered right or wrong, and we were loved before we existed. We were simply loved and still loved to this day. We can rest in the grace of God's love because it is His grace to give us, and not ours to earn. Just because we are being corrected by God does not remove His grace toward us. The opposite would be true because God corrects those He loves. Prov. 3:12 **For whom the LORD loves he corrects; even as a father the son in whom he delights**. The abundant grace God has poured out on us is not fragile but carries a strength of holy integrity that cannot be taken from us by any battle or devious plan the enemy of our soul would conjure up in his pathetic attempt at playing god. Isa. 54:17 **No weapon that is formed against you will prosper; and you will condemn every tongue that rises against you in judgment. This is the heritage of the servants of the LORD, and their righteousness which is of me," says the LORD**. The gracious favour the Lord has been nurturing within us cannot be removed by anything outside of our being.

The Lord's eternal grace is at work within us and has become an inner lining of our soul which will help us be disciplined in grace.

We, the sons and daughters of the Lord, are the result of God's generous grace. God will keep pouring His favour on us for a testimony of God's goodness in us. Acts 4:33 **And with great power gave the apostles witness of the resurrection of the Lord Jesus: and great grace was upon them all**. We sometimes think that when we commit a great wrong the Lord's grace stops flowing. Not so! Saul was persecuting Christians and God's grace was extended to Saul on his way to Damascus. God's grace with conviction had such a profound effect on Saul he became a Christian and immediately changed his message. Grace had given Saul the discipline he needed to go forth in his ministry.

I am not advocating that everyone run out and act helter-skelter and throw our holiness to the wind. I do not act right to earn God's grace. I let grace discipline my heart because I have God's gift of grace working in me. Eph. 2:8 **For by grace are** ye saved through faith; and that not of yourselves: it is the gift of God: 9 **Not of works, lest any man should boast**. As long as we live on this earth we will need redemptive improvement in our hearts. Being disciplined in the grace of God will help us walk in the Spirit of the Lord's love. I do not believe we have scratched the surface of grace and our understanding of it. I think there will be an eternity of learning as to how wonderful the Lord's graciousness toward us is. Grace is not a weak and fragile gift of God that will not stand up to the sins of the human race. Grace is much stronger than what we have been presenting it as.

The marvel and epitome of grace is its ability to change a lost soul, a sick person, or someone with a depressed spirit into a fully living born-again person of God who loves the very life they have. 2Thes. 1:12 **That the name of our Lord Jesus Christ may be glorified in you, and ye in him, according to the grace of our God and the Lord Jesus Christ**. Our life can be turned right around from the edge of the pit of hell to the lofty heights of God's joy. We can be steadfastly headed for destruction, and within a moment of time grace can rescue us for a life with a God-given purpose. Titus 2:11 **For the grace of God that bringeth salvation hath appeared to all men**. We can be assured and feel safe in the discipline of God's loving grace. We can trust the discipline of God's grace to lead us to the love of the Father.

Having Grace For Yourself

For many Christians, self-compassion is one of the hardest blessings from God to accept and put into practice. Having or giving grace to ourselves can be emotionally problematic when shame and regret are at the forefront of a person's mind. In theory, Christians know they are saved and are loved, but in their hearts there is often a battle of belief because everyone knows their secret shortcomings. This can bring out anger and resentment towards ourselves and could leave room for the enemy of our soul to molest our minds. Satan will use people's hurts and bad memories to keep them off balance by pointing out they are not doing enough for the Lord, and therefore, they should not expect any love or rest from God until a greater sacrifice is given of themselves. Notice that when Satan cannot tempt you to sin, he changes tactics and starts accusing you of not measuring up to God's standard of service that you are doing in the Lord's Kingdom. The weapons most used in the battle for our mind are lies of great invention and accusations. Jesus' sacrifice on the cross has given us all the grace we need and could ever want. Yes, by grace we are saved; therefore, we need to extend that grace to ourselves as well as others.

The discipline it takes to extend God's grace upon ourselves can be a battle for some because of the self-condemnation prevalent among those who have a hard time believing that God loves them. My friend Carolyn says, "Self-compassion is the farthest thing from our hearts when we are wrestling with traumas, sins, and hurtful memories of our past. We end up striving for God's love because we do not feel we deserve His love nor deserve to grant our lives the grace God has already given us. What a mess we make of this beautiful gift God gave us." Heb. 4:15 **For we do not have a high priest who is unable to sympathize with our weaknesses, but one who in every respect has been tempted as we are, yet without sin. 16 Let us then with confidence draw near to the throne of grace, that we may receive mercy and find grace to help in time of need.**

This is often an area that firstborns wrestle with. A few of my friends and I are firstborns in our families, and we have discussed at length the difficulty of disciplining our hearts to accept what God says about us. We have noticed that firstborns can easily disqualify themselves from accepting grace because many firstborns often seek approval and recognition plus have the need to be liked. In many cases when firstborns were young, they became stuck in their emotions, because they were given a lot of the responsibility in the family. The unnatural expectations that were placed upon them were difficult to fulfill at best, and impossible most of the time. Firstborns were often blamed for a lot of what their siblings did wrong and any 'thank yous' for what they had done right, were far and between the accusations of failure. All these memories need the discipline of mind and heart to be placed under the blood of Jesus' sacrifice. We all need to find our approval in God so that we can receive grace for ourselves and rest in the fact that Jesus procured God's approval for us on the cross.

I am not creating a law or saying this is a firstborn's cross to bear, nor am I saying they are the only ones suffering trauma. This is an observation that is common among firstborns. Most people have their emotional pains to bear and overcome. Everyone needs to bring their messed up thoughts and self-image issues to the cross so that they may receive the healing grace that Jesus won for us all. The discipline of coming to the cross regularly is what will heal our lives from the traumas of our past. We need to be gracious to others and ourselves so that the work of grace can work its miracles in our hearts.

Other Thoughts

When we become born-again Christians, we take on the new nature of Christ within us, and we become kings and priests of the Lord. Rev. 1:6a **And hath made us kings and priests unto God and his Father.** As kings, we rule with righteousness toward all people and as priests, we minister with grace toward all people on behalf of our Lord and Saviour Jesus Christ. Prov. 22:11 **He who loves purity of heart, and has grace on his lips, The king will be his friend.** I was able to experience this type of friendship with the Lord's grace. I saw firsthand the blessing of living and ministering from a position of grace toward my brothers, sisters, coworkers, family, and everyone I came across. I noticed that there would be a miracle manifested within seconds, minutes, and days of offering grace to everyone who needed grace. I found a verse that liberated my heart and the simplicity of its words was pure joy. Acts 14:3 **Long time, therefore, abode they speaking boldly in the Lord, which gave testimony unto the word of his grace, and granted signs and wonders to be done by their hands.** The words in this verse that touched my spirit were, "Which gave testimony unto the word of his grace."

Paul and his ministry team ministered the word of the Lord's grace. What was the result of this word of grace ministered? The Word says, "Granted signs and wonders to be done by their hands." I asked God if it could be this simple and I immediately started practising what I had received through the illumination of this word and the results were immediate. Signs and wonders began manifesting all around my everyday life. I noticed that this was what Jesus was doing when He walked with His disciples in the everyday life of their ministry because Jesus was full of grace and truth. John 1:14 **And the Word was made flesh, and dwelt among us, and we beheld his glory, the glory as of the only begotten of the Father, full of grace and truth.** 16 **And of His fullness have all we received, and grace for grace.** 17 **For the law was given by Moses, but grace and truth came by Jesus Christ.** Whenever Jesus did anything, He did it from a position of grace first then truth to seal His love toward the people.

The woman caught in adultery, Jesus said to her, "Neither do I condemn thee: go, and sin no more." The grace was no condemnation, and the truth was go and sin no more. The leper in the synagogue, Jesus says, "I will; be thou clean, but go thy way, shew thyself to the priest." The grace was the cleansing of leprosy, and the truth was to show the cleansing to the priest.

Jairus' daughter had died, and Jesus said, "I say unto thee, arise, and commanded that something should be given her to eat." The grace was healing her from death, and the truth was to give her something to eat. In these true stories, grace was offered to deal with a miracle needed in life, and the truth was given because truth is needed to keep going on in life. We offer grace because grace has been given to us, and we minister the truth because the truth of grace will set everyone who receives it free. Grace for grace. What an amazing grace we have been given. Eph. 2:8 **For by grace are ye saved through faith; and that not of yourselves: it is the gift of God:** 9 **Not of works, lest any man should boast.** This grace that we have been given, by faith, is ours to give so that signs and wonders would follow. I love the truth of His grace. Amen.

Part Two
Discipline In God's Word

The Word of God is alive. John 1:1 **In the beginning was the Word, and the Word was with God, and the Word was God**. The living Word is God manifested in the flesh. Jesus the Saviour of the world was given to us by our Heavenly Father. John 1:14 **The Word became flesh and made his dwelling among us. We have seen His glory, the glory of the one and only Son, who came from the Father, full of grace and truth**. The Rhema of God's Word brings life to those who believe in it, and apply it to their lives. The power of God's Word cannot be overemphasized because we do not fully grasp the awesomeness of the Word's capability to bring God and man together in the Spirit. Not only can we become disciplined in being led by the Spirit of God, we can grow in the power of its infinite grace. Heb. 4:12 **For the word of God is alive and powerful. It is sharper than the sharpest two-edged sword, cutting between soul and spirit, between joint and marrow. It exposes our innermost thoughts and desires**.

There is nothing so heart-healing as hearing the right word at the right time. In that moment of hearing a word of blessing, deliverance or assurance, we then know that we know God has heard our heart's cry and there is a peace that is beyond words of explanation that settles our hearts. Phil. 4:7 **And the peace of God, which passes all understanding, shall keep your hearts and minds through Christ Jesus**. It is always nice to receive that fulfilling word when we are in need, but just as nice to be the one giving it out and doing it from a heart of blessing. There is an amazing side factor of blessing that happens when someone gives out a gracious encouragement or a kind action. The one who needed a word in season gets blessed, and the one who gave it away also gets blessed, but most interesting is if anyone sees this blessing taking place between the giver and recipient they also get blessed. Talk about paying it forward. This blessed result has a compounding effect. Blessing upon blessing goes out and will not come back empty. Isa. 55:11 **So shall my word be that goes forth out of my mouth: it shall not return unto me void, but it shall accomplish that which I please, and it shall prosper in the thing whereto I sent it**. How hard is it to say something encouraging to anyone? How much discipline does it take to extend a gracious hand on God's behalf?

We are fortunate to have the Word of God within our reach. At any moment of the day, we can soak in its life-giving force to renew our mind to the truth of what God says about us and how much He loves us. Jer. 31:3 **The LORD appeared to us in the past, saying: "I have loved you with an everlasting love; I have drawn you with unfailing kindness**. The Word truly does give life and along with that gift of life comes our need to keep on being diligent in studying and referring to the Lord's Word regularly. 2Tim. 2:15 **Study and do your best to present yourself to God-approved, a workman tested by trial who has no reason to be ashamed, accurately handling and skillfully teaching the word of truth**. The enemy of our soul does not take days off from attacking and accusing us of every lie there is. We need to remain disciplined in growing and exceling within our faith through God's Word.

Remain disciplined in loving God's Word. Don't become careless with it and end up in a place where you become bitter and resentful of the Lord's instruction. Prov. 13:13 **Whoso despises the word shall be destroyed: but he that fears the commandment shall be rewarded**. To despise means: "To regard as negligible, worthless, distasteful, or to look down on with contempt." To despise the written Word of God is to despise Jesus; even if you do not like what I am saying, this is true. My late Pastor Arnold Kalamen often said, "If Jesus is not Lord of all, He is not Lord at all." How precious is the Word of God. We have free access to its God-inspired instructions for our lives every minute and day if we want it. This gift exists because of the sacrifice of the early believers from our Christian history. John 4:37 **And herein is that saying true, One sows, and another reaps.** 38 **I sent you to reap that whereon ye bestowed no labour: other men laboured, and ye are entered into their labours**.

Our forerunners in the faith paid for the bible with their lives and today we can live in the blessing of the Word of the Lord because of those sacrifices. To despise this living Word is an indictment against our responsibility and stewardship of this good news message for our times. Pastor Robert Morris says, "God tests our faith with the prophetic Word, then God tests our character with the written Word." If we do not take the written Word of God to heart and allow that instructional word to cleanse and direct us forward, we will not fulfill our destiny God has purposed for us. Thomas Edison said, "Vision without execution is just hallucination." The Lord said it this way in James 2:20b **That faith without works is dead**. We must put our faith in the Word that points to Jesus whom God gave us, because He is the only way we will get direction from God. Heb. 1:1 **God, who at sundry times and in divers manners spake in time past unto the fathers by the prophets, 2 Hath in these last days spoken unto us by his Son, whom he hath appointed heir of all things, by whom also he made the worlds**.

After the book of Malachi was written, there are approximately four hundred years of God's voice being silent. Man finally hears God speak again at the baptism of Jesus and His transfiguration where God says, Luke 9:35 **And there came a voice out of the cloud, saying, This is my beloved Son: hear him**. That was all God said, "Hear Him." What elaboration is needed here? Hear Him, listen to Him, believe what He says, and have faith in Him. Jesus is the Word of God and God's living Word is in us to fulfill the holy will of the Father. 1John 5:11 **And this is the record,** that **God hath given to us eternal life, and this life is in his Son**. I love the Word of God and the Word loves me. 1Cor. 3:23 **And ye are Christ's; and Christ is God's**.

Discipline In Reading The Context Of God's Word

When God's Word is taken out of context, we can end up with cults forming in the name of spirituality. Anyone can make the Bible say anything they want it to say, to allow themselves to live in the sin or lifestyle of their choice. When I am asked, "Why are there so many cults and divisions in the world church?" The answer comes down to basics. The hermeneutics and laws of interpretation are ignored to suit the goals of certain people. Whether the motivation is to scam parishioners out of their money or fulfill an egoistic power-hungry quest to control people's hearts for self-worship, the laws of scriptural interpretation are disregarded which allows the said cult to flourish.

The context of the word is normally straightforward, and if a person's heart is sincere in seeking God, then God will ensure the revelatory meaning of the Word that has been read, will get through to the reader's heart. The Apostle Paul points out that there should be more than one example of context to draw from. 2Cor. 13:1b **In the mouth of two or three witnesses shall every word be established**. We have seen whole sects evolve out of one scripture taken out of context. A Bible verse that comes to mind that has become the foundation of a circus act in some religious gatherings is Mark 16:18 **They will be able to handle snakes with safety, and if they drink anything poisonous, it won't hurt them. They will be able to place their hands on the sick, and they will be healed**.

I will use this example because this faction of believers has been exposed by people who were once in this group and have explained how the trickery works. The crazed snake handlers try to prove their faith by stepping into a snake pit while screaming in a King James dialect, the scripture being used out of context, plus putting on a show for the faithful. Interviews with people who have come out of this sect have explained that the rattlesnakes have had their venom squeezed out and the handlers have become immune through small doses of the venom over time. This deception has caused a whole group of believers to set their hearts on the misinterpretation of one verse.

Are there other scriptures in the Bible that say to go out and pick up poisonous snakes? Not that I can find. There is an account of the Apostle Paul being bitten by a viper, and to the astonishment of the villagers, Paul shakes the snake off and he is not harmed. Acts 28:5 **But Paul shook off the snake into the fire and was unharmed**. Now, this scripture brings context to the one in Mark 16:18a **They will be able to handle snakes with safety**. It is God's protection from the snake that is being explained and not the command to go out and tempt the Lord by looking for dangerous snakes to cuddle up with. Does this gameshow atmosphere bring glory to God? This is only my opinion, but I think it brings tears to the Godhead, but it also reinforces the love that God has for this lost world. His amazing grace will reach down and touch anyone who looks to Him for salvation and that includes the scammers, conmen, the fools and sinners of all kinds.

Are there many other examples of scriptures being taken out of context? There are hundreds of accounts that go on day by day. The damage that this type of scriptural misinterpretation can have on the souls who fall for the trappings and trickery can last a lifetime once the betrayal is realized. Finding the context of scripture is paramount, and proclaiming the importance of remaining disciplined in following the Lord through His inspired Word is our duty. We can do better. We need to ask the Holy Spirit during our times of reading and studying God's Word, to bring the context to our hearts so that we may walk in the assurance of our salvation.

Norm Sawyer said, "As you become disciplined in God's love you become wiser in faith."

Part Three
Discipline In Our Faith

Jeremiah 2:13 For my people have committed a double evil: They have abandoned me, the fountain of living water, and dug cisterns for themselves —cracked cisterns that cannot hold water.

The gospel of convenience has become popular for the whims that flow through people's hearts in these times of uncertainty. When someone does not agree with an instructional scripture they do not like, or do not want to sacrifice any comfort that the scripture might demand of them, they simply say, "Well, I'm not sure if that interpretation of that scripture is of God." They also say things like, "This section of the New Testament was added years later after the first church started and before the Bible's canonization was put together. How can I trust what might not be the word of God?" Even though the Word says that all scripture is divinely inspired to help correct our lives, these gainsayers keep up the pretence of wanting what God has for them but are not willing to trust that God will direct them to righteousness in Christ. 1Tim. 3:16 **All Scripture is inspired by God and is useful to teach us what is true and to make us realize what is wrong in our lives**.

The Word of Faith corrects us when we are wrong and teaches us to do what is right. How convenient to cherry-pick what one wants to believe so that one can remain a non-participant in the maturity of their soul. How can anyone have a disciplined faith if they are second-guessing every other scripture as to whether it is divinely inspired or not? The fear of error is not a reason to stop looking for the truth concerning Jesus our Saviour. There comes a time when we will need to trust that God speaks to us through His revealed Word, because without faith at work in our hearts, it is impossible to please God. Heb. 11:6 **And without faith it is impossible to please God, because anyone who comes to Him must believe that He exists and that He rewards those who earnestly seek Him**. We must believe that He exists and that He rewards those who seek Him. Why seek a God you have no faith in? This is what an undisciplined person does. They look for answers with very little expectation of finding the answers for their lives, and then when things fall apart they claim that faith does not work. That is not faith, but rather it is unbelief disguised as faith or in most cases fatalism. Religious activity involving rote rituals may not bring the results that a disciplined heart focused on a relationship with Christ can bring to our souls when faith is activated.

What is and how do we develop a discipline in the faith that comes through receiving Jesus Christ as Lord? We study the Word of God so that our spirits are renewed toward what the Holy Spirit is teaching us, and we believe the love God has for us. Rom. 10:7 **So faith is from hearing, and hearing through the word of Christ**. When we use our faith in accepting the love God has for us, we will know without doubt that we are loved. 1John 4:16 **And we have known and believed the love that God hath to us. God is love; and he that dwelleth in love dwelleth in God, and God in him**. Being confident in the love of God will bolster our resolve to believe in God's perfect will for our lives and that He wants a loving relationship with us. We need confidence in God to know that He is for us, and there is nothing that can take away His love that He freely gives us every moment of the day. 1John 5:14 **This is the confidence we have in approaching God: that if we ask anything according to his will, he hears us. 15 And if we know that He hears us—whatever we ask—we know that we have what we asked of Him**. One becomes free in their faith when one is disciplined in their faith. Being disciplined brings freedom to our souls and lives.

Other Thoughts

As believing saints and disciples of Jesus, we should be the happiest people on earth. By the grace of God, we who are the children of our Lord can bring hope to those who have lost their way in this ever-changing world. After all, we do have the Godhead living within our being, and the ability to be a heavenly encouragement. These Godly blessings should be flowing out of our lives. Philemon 1:7 **For I have great joy and encouragement from your love, because the hearts of the saints have been refreshed through you, brother.** Sometimes, we the saints of the Lord, can become battle-weary and begin to lose the vision that was once clear and attainable in our hearts. Tiredness in our soul can affect our faith and walk with God. Therefore, we have to choose to turn our faith back on. Gal. 6:9 **And let us not be weary in well doing: for in due season we shall reap, if we faint not.** It is not up to your pastor, spouse, friend, or leader to get your faith working again—it is up to you and God. Where the aforementioned people can be helpful, is after they have chosen to turn their faith back on, they can move forward in the will of God. By praying and asking God for help and strength, God can use these people to spark a new desire to become disciplined in their faith.

God instructed Samuel the prophet to anoint David as the future king of Israel. Time moved on and now David had conquered and killed the giant Goliath. He was on the heavenly fast-track for kingdom promotion. He was married to King Saul's daughter and living the good life in the palace. What could go wrong? Everything went wrong. David was falsely accused of treason and conspiracy. It was said he wanted to take the kingdom from Saul. He ended up a hunted man and running for his life. Now, having to live in caves and on the outskirts of villages in the hillsides, he had become a fugitive. David must have prayed to God, and said, "I thought Samuel said I would be the king of Israel. I must have misunderstood. What did I do to deserve all this calamity in my life?" David had to encourage himself in the Lord and decide to turn his faith back on. He travelled to the town of Nob, and there, he was given Goliath's sword. 1Sam. 21:9 **"The priest replied, "The sword of Goliath the Philistine, whom you killed in the Valley of Elah, is here, wrapped in a cloth behind the ephod. If you want to take it for yourself, then take it, for there isn't another one here." "There's none like it!" David said. "Give it to me."**

God knows exactly what we need and when we need it. Just as David's faith needed encouragement, God reminded him of who he was, and that his future was still in God's hands. The sword David used to cut off Goliath's head was a timely reminder of all the victories that David had gone through. David also remembered that the prophecies that had been spoken over him were still true and an inspiration to turn his faith back on. He was walking through the wilderness of his life, but God met him and reminded him of the vision and promise for his life.

Now, David could say with courage: Psalm 63:9 **But those who intend to destroy my life will go into the depths of the earth. 10 They will be given over to the power of the sword; they will become a meal for jackals.**

If gloominess and sadness have replaced your saintly shout in the Lord, then develop a discipline in God's Word and turn your faith back on. God knows what you need and that your strength will come through the joy of the Lord and faith in His name. Neh. 8:10b **For the joy of the LORD is your strength.** What have you let go of that was once the vision of God for your life? How have you let the circumstances of life take your call, strength, and ministry away from the forefront of your mind and spirit? Get your discipline of faith working again and get with God's eternal vision for your life.

We can count on God to preserve the dreams He sowed in our hearts when He created us. As saints in the Lord, we stay on the path God has laid out for us so that our life's purpose may be fulfilled. Prov.

2:8 **He guards the paths of justice, and preserves the way of His saints**. There will be times when we fail, but our faith in the Lord can lift us above the failure and put the shout of victory back in our hearts. As saints in Christ, we can help many overcome the sadness that is prevalent in this world. May our God remind us of the giants we have slain and the victories we have won in the Lord's name. Yes, we are more than conquerors, through Christ, who gives us the victory.

Part Four
Discipline In Obedience

Matthew 13:13 In them is fulfilled the prophecy of Isaiah: "'You will be ever hearing but never understanding; you will be ever seeing but never perceiving. 15 For this people's heart has become

calloused; they hardly hear with their ears, and they have closed their eyes. Otherwise they might see with their eyes, hear with their ears, understand with their hearts and turn, and I would heal them.'

What I notice in the above Scripture that refers to Isaiah's prophecy, is how Jesus explains that even though the people have eyes and ears, they will not be able to see, hear, or understand, because the illumination of hearing and seeing what God is saying, only comes to our hearts when we WANT to obey God. Then God allows our hearts to understand His Word. I know it sounds too simple and it's like discovering cold water, but it makes sense why many Christians are not growing. They really don't want to obey God because they are living on the premise that they have to obey God. Resulting in a pablum diet of Christianese.

Some of my friends who are pastors often ask, "Why is it that a lot of the parishioners get to a certain place of maturity and then stop growing and remain in that same place of spiritual existence for the longest time?" The answer might be too simple. Many people stop growing because they are afraid God is going to ask them to do something they do not want to do, therefore, remaining in a place where they are saved through Christ's sacrifice but immature to be counted on to do what God wants. Thus they remain in a position of disobedience and wonder why life is difficult.

If these people were disciplined in their obedience, they would soon realize that when God asks them to do something for Him, He will provide the means and strength to pull it off. One of the fears I have heard is, "What if God wants me to go and be a missionary in China?" News break: Why would God send you to China when you can't even keep your room clean? Why would He give you eternal responsibility in another country when you are not responsible for getting your garage cleaned up, or setting your home in order? Why would he ask you to bring your bad habits to another country and make the place worse than it is because Jesus is not a revelation in that nation? Discipline in obedience to our daily devotional life in Christ is crucial to a strong relationship with our Lord and the plans for His kingdom.

Remaining just outside of the maturity needed to find God's will for your life is not a fulfilling life in Christ, it is a miserable existence in religiosity and boredom.In most cases, the church attendance of those who remain in this state of ecclesiastical existence and low-value spiritual growth, ends up creating hearts and souls that are vulnerable and weak to Satan's tormenting attacks. Eph. 4:27 **Neither give place to the devil**. How can one raise a standard of righteousness when they are having a hard time believing they are the righteousness of God through Christ? No, this is not a way to remain safe so to speak in your relationship with God, it is a slow death waiting to happen. Discipline in our obedience is the key to rising above the fears of man, and the taunting lies of the enemy.

Trust the Lord to know our frame and abilities. The Lord will use us where He created us to be usable. Psalm 103:14 **For he knows how we are formed,**

He remembers that we are dust. Our purpose in life will develop as we obey the voice and Word of the Lord, and then when we hear His instruction, we will need to obey by faith and head in the direction of the said instruction. Our discipline in obedience to the will and heart of God will be required for the length of our lives and time on this earth. There are no long weekends or holidays from walking with the Lord as we are yoked to Him through Christ. If the Lord is not taking time off from His righteous and obedient position of existence, then we too need to live within His paradigm of eternity. That is the only place we will find rest.

I Choose To Obey

Even though obedience is a choice, it still takes discipline to be obedient. If our hearts are not subject to the Lordship of Jesus, it does not take long before we are drifting toward doing our own thing. Our resolve to walk in the leading of the Lord will wear down if we do not apply the disciplines we learned in the Word of God. As many have experienced, it does not take much parting from God's truth to drift. We need to understand that it does not take much to realize one needs to repent and change our mind when God points out that we are walking in the wrong direction. However, we do need to stop and turn at that point of knowing right from wrong. The story of the two sons making a choice of obedience that Jesus taught, shows us the words we speak and the choices we make will eventually show what our character truly is. Matt. 21:28 **"What do you think? There was a man who had two sons. He went to the first and said, 'Son, go and work today in the vineyard.' 29 'I will not,' he answered, but later he changed his mind and went. 30 "Then the father went to the other son and said the same thing. He answered, 'I will, sir,' but he did not go. 31a "Which of the two did what his father wanted?" "The first,"** they answered.

When we live a life where discipline is a guiding beacon, we can turn around quickly when we realize we made the wrong move. Discipline's capacity to teach us as we use it to guide our actions is profound and reliable. Plus, we have the added blessing that God will help us become disciplined in the grace, laws, and attributes of God. His will is that we listen to His council and that we obey His Word so that we may live a life of gratefulness, health, holy strength and honour. Ex. 15:26 **And He said, "If you will listen carefully to the voice of the LORD your God, and do what is right in His sight, and listen to His commandments, and keep all His statutes, I will put none of the diseases on you which I have put on the Egyptians; for I, the LORD, am your healer."** The far-reaching health that comes through the healing Word of God will be a strong deterrent from the attack of the enemy who hates everything that is God-centered. The healing of our body, soul, and spirit will help us be who God created us to be in this lost and often evil world.

One of the terrible disorders that have become prevalent in our day is mental illness and manic depression. If ever there was a place for the art of discipline it would be in the area of the mind where learning how to take our thoughts captive and filter them through the washing and cleansing Word of God is a discipline that would heal countless amounts of suffering people. However, the choice to obey the instructions of the Lord will still need to be a choice of will. Why is obedience to the leading of the Holy Spirit so crucial for our survival and the survival of our future generations? One of the reasons is that hopefully, we will raise our children to walk in the council of God. Duet. 30:19 **I call heaven and earth to witness against you today, that I have placed before you life and death, the blessing and the curse. So choose life in order that you may live, you and your descendants**.

Much of the world's citizenry has bought into the devil's lie that disobedience to God and any law-abiding authority is a deliberate attempt to take away their freedom. The devil promotes that everyone should just go ahead and do their own thing to be really free. But the results of this practiced behaviour is evident in the chaos and hate that is running rampant throughout the world. No one is free when everyone is selfishly taking your freedom to have their own way. Everyone loses when there are no laws to live by.

Discipline In Morality

Discipline in one's morality is one of the hardest arrears in this fast-changing life to keep up with. The goalpost of morality from the world's perspective is changing all the time. The revolving changes and the acceptance of sin in society eventually make their way into the church and the debate is on. The personal opinions of many become the standard of what they think should be allowed is skewed because their statements of "I know the Bible says that, but I believe, and I know the Word of God says that, but I think," become the standard of their expectation and they want the church to accept their modern interpretation of what is considered a sin. Meanwhile, God's standards and plumline for living and guiding our lives, become the battleground. This is when the disciple of moral choices according to what the Spirit of God is saying to your soul becomes the choice to make.

You will hear people say, "Follow your heart." This may sound quaint and even philosophically helpful, but the Word of God makes it clear that the heart is the most deceptive and wicked thing, and cannot be trusted. Jer. 17:9 **The human heart is the most deceitful of all things, and desperately wicked. Who really knows how bad it is?** We need the discernment of the Holy Spirit to declare to our soul what sin is and what is not iniquitous behaviour. Just because someone feels they have the right to rewrite scripture to suit their sin does not make it right or acceptable to

God. The sons of Aaron decided to follow their hearts when they were performing their priestly duties. Whenever incense was offered to the Lord, the only fire the priests were commanded to use was that from the altar of burnt offering. Aaron's sons thought that using their idea of which fire was acceptable was good enough and they could burn incense the way they interpreted the law. However, this brought about a quick judgment from God, and they were killed. Lev. 10:2 **So fire blazed forth from the LORD's presence and burned them up, and they died there before the LORD**. Nadab and Abihu's personal fire killed them. In the same way today, many are dying a slow death in the church as they apply their personal fires and interpretations to the Word of God to suit their sins of choice.

Before anyone could voice their opinion as to what God had done to Nadab and Abihu, God said to Moses: Lev. 10:6 **Then Moses said to Aaron and his sons Eleazar and Ithamar, "Do not show grief by leaving your hair uncombed**

or by tearing your clothes. If you do, you will die, and the LORD's anger will strike the whole community of Israel. However, the rest of the Israelites, your relatives, may mourn because of the LORD's fiery destruction of Nadab and Abihu. This would be harsh if we had to encounter the true cost of our big mouths and sin. However, through Christ our Lord there is grace for us. Aaron and his priestly ministers could not voice their grief by mourning what God had done to Aaron's sons. Our personal fires or beliefs per se do not matter in the light of what the Lord says is morally acceptable. Our ability to be disciplined in making moral choices should be based on what the Word of God says, and not upon the whims and feelings of an unprincipled and manipulative society. I agree that in this overindulgent world, it is becoming difficult to remain forthright and pure of heart, especially when anything imaginable is being offered every hour of the day and in any quantity a person can want. The choice to let things slip can become a small habit at first, but in no time at all, these choices can become a Goliath monster that needs taking down and the fight may be more than some can handle. Wouldn't it be better to not have allowed the slipping to start in the first place? Remain disciplined in your heart and your morals will follow.

Discipline In Prayer

When I'm asked how much time I spend in prayer each day, it becomes a difficult question to answer as God's Word says to pray without ceasing. 1Thes. 5:17 **Pray without ceasing**. I do not measure in minutes the amount of time communing with my Lord, because I don't have a specific set of rules for the length of time praying. As the Lord instructed His disciples, "When you pray, say Our Father." Once a person sincerely says "Our Father, Holy is your name," the time is not the issue but what our Father instructs us to do becomes the revelatory standard for the day. What I notice is that the time between prayers and the continual dislodging in heart with the Lord, is what carries me through the day and this is the discipline I am after for the nurturing of my soul and heart.

I believe some seasons will require longer periods of time in prayer to overcome the burdens of life and death, as these events may be placed upon one's heart by the Holy Spirit. There are many times when praying in the Spirit for breakthroughs for family, church, or national crises may be needed to find the victory that will deliver the people from the assault of the enemy. This is what the body of Christ is built to do—to lift each other into the presence of God and by faith call for the Lord's help in a helpless situation. Acts 4:29 **And now, Lord, look upon their threats and grant to your servants to continue to speak your word with all boldness,** 30 **while you stretch out your hand to heal, and signs and wonders are performed through the name of your holy servant Jesus**. Part of the discipline in our prayer life is to know the times and types of prayer to pray forth.

Whether it is imprecatory prayers for justice or claiming the souls of the lost, we need to discern when and how to pray. When I am asked to pray for any situation, I do it on the spot and within moments later I am talking to God again asking Him to hear my words and consider my meditation. Psalm 5:1 **Give ear to my words, O LORD, consider my meditation**. My meditation on God becomes a prayer, and the discipline needed to keep my mind and thoughts toward His love for me is needed because this keeps me coming back. This is a discipline that is needed in the body of Christ.

This is what my pastor reminded me of concerning prayer. He said, "In any conversation, our time yields to the more important person, and in this context, it is the Lord. He does the talking: my posture is to listen. Prayer to me is 99% listening to God speak, and 1% talking." This may be hard for some people to be disciplined to do, only having 1% of the dialogue. However, we need to listen to what the Spirit is saying and not be talking over what He is saying. Walking daily with God is communing with God. Regardless of the problems and mess one might be in, the only way through the mess is to keep close to Jesus and find the Word of God that allows us to reason through the mess as we look for God's forgiveness. Isa. 1:18 **Come now, let us reason together, says the LORD: though your sins are like scarlet, they shall be as white as snow; though they are red like crimson, they shall become like wool**. How can one hear from God when one is avoiding God's loving scrutiny of our hearts? Prayer can lead us to a willingness to repent. No wonder Satan is hell-bent on distracting us from praying for solutions in our lives. The devil would rather have us looking at the problems and wringing our hands over the helplessness of it all. No, Saints! We were created to breathe, live, and talk with our Creator. Acts 17:28a **For in Him we live, and move, and have our being**. We must develop the discipline and willingness to commune with the Lord at all times. Discipline in prayer brings freedom to our souls.

Other Thoughts

Proverbs 12:25 Anxiety in a person's heart weighs it down, but a good word cheers it up.

Teresa of Ávila said, "More tears are shed over answered prayers than unanswered ones."

Praying God's will for your life can be uncomfortable. God might ask you to do something that seems to be an enormous request. Nonetheless, it has been asked. When Jesus was praying in the garden of Gethsemane, it was not a pleasant time. It was a time to come to grips with why Jesus came to earth. Luke 22:42b **Nevertheless, not my will, but yours, be done**. The courage it took for Jesus to say, "Your will be done" was immense. God may ask you to forgive someone for doing something so heinous and brutal, even though the brutality affected your life. The Lord may ask you to sacrifice something that means so much to you. No matter the degree of difficulty in the natural, we still have to come to God in prayer, and it may be very uncomfortable. God is moved by faith and not the hardships we are going through. Heb. 11:6 **But without faith it is impossible to please him: for he that cometh to God must believe that he is, and that he is a rewarder of them that diligently seek him**.

I had a discussion with my uncle who is having a hard time forgiving two people in his life. One of them is dead, and the other is alive. The interesting thing is that the one who is dead has so much power over my uncle's life, even though this person is no longer on this earth. The bitterness and resentment my uncle is feeling are being controlled by someone long in the grave. My uncle was being weighed down in anxiety because he could not forgive the past. Prov. 12:25a **Anxiety in a person's heart weighs it down**. I explained to him—as uncomfortable as it is, he is going to have to forgive the actions that were done to him many years ago. God was asking him to forgive a dead man so that my uncle could be set free to go on living. "This is not an easy prayer," he said. The discomfort came when it was clear that my uncle wanted grace for himself but the judgment of God on those who had hurt him. He only started to get his peace when he asked God to help him forgive the living and the dead. I heard someone say, "What the tongue promises, the body must follow." If the tongue forgives, the body, soul, and mind will heal.

We wouldn't need a Saviour if we could do all these hard things on our own. We need our Lord's help in all our lives and all that we do. Phil. 4:6 **Do not be anxious about anything, but in every situation, by prayer and petition, with thanksgiving, present your requests to God**. Whether we need deliverance from sin we participate in regularly, or we are dealing with a monstrous challenge in our life, we need to get down to some prayer time with the Lord no matter how uncomfortable it seems.

When Daniel was in the lion's den, it

was not a comfortable place to pray from or situation to be in. But all he could do was pray. When Jonah was in the belly of the great fish, it was most definitely not a comfortable place to pray or be in. But, again, what choice did Jonah have but to pray? Jonah 2:1 **Then Jonah prayed to the LORD his God from the belly of the fish**. After being whipped and chained in the deepest dungeon, Paul and Silas prayed and praised God in the discomfort of their pain and humiliation. These people prayed disciplined prayers in uncomfortable times but ended up in the comfort of the Holy Spirit.

Our Heavenly Father may be asking us to do some hard things. It will take discipline of heart to pray and we may not have a nice comfortable closet to pray in. We may be in the depths of our despair, pain, or suffering. The discomfort might even be palpable. Nonetheless, what else are we going to do? Psalm 121:1 **I look up to the mountains— does my help come from there? 2 My help comes from the LORD, who made heaven and**

earth! That is it, saints. We keep looking to God in all our trials and hard times. We may be in a place of uncomfortable prayer because of a terrible situation. But when a good anointed Word comes from God, our hearts will lose the anxiety that weighed it down. We will rise in the confidence of our God who loves us. 1John 5:14 **And this is the confidence that we have in him, that, if we ask any thing according to his will, he heareth us: 15 and if we know that he hear us, whatsoever we ask, we know that we have the petitions that we desired of him**. Being disciplined in prayer is simply continually talking with God about everything we are doing in life.

Norm Sawyer said, "Discipline is a cruel master, but a necessary companion."

Part Five
Discipline In Health

The Stroke And The Light

On the evening of August 2nd. 2014 I suffered a Transient Ischemic Attack (TIA). I was crouched low trying to put a frying pan away in a bottom cabinet and came up too fast and felt a dizzy spell, but when I saw a strange flash in the depth of my eyes, it got scary. The counter seemed to split into two images and would not line up. I then lost control of my right arm and started slurring my words while hanging onto the counter, slowly headed for the floor. There was a trapped feeling in my mind because what I wanted to do would not work. I kept trying to put a pan lid away but my right arm would not go in the direction I wanted. I felt a heat-wave start to go through my head and I thought, "I am having a stroke." I called my wife who had just asked if I was OK. I said, "Nooooo,"while slurring. "I thhhink I'mmm haavving a strooookkke," came out of my mouth in slow motion. My wide-eyed wife jumped up and started to pray out loud. "IN JESUS' NAME!!!!" Over and over again she kept saying His name. Acts 4:12 **Neither is there salvation in any other: for there is none other name under heaven given among men, whereby we must be saved**. That was the first wave of the attack. I felt like my face was melting away, and had slackened into a droop. My wife said my face had turned pure white.

I felt a terrible burning feeling in my brain and I went to my knees as my vision continued to be in a split screen view so to speak, and then as the Apostle Paul says, 2Cor. 12:3 **And I know that this man was**

caught up into paradise — whether in the
body or out of the body I do not know,
God knows. Similarly whether in the body
or out of the body I do not know, but God
knows. Whether I died for milliseconds or
moments I do not know, but God knows as I
encountered the bright white light of God's
overwhelming love. The inspiring feelings
of the Lord's cleansing righteousness and
the pureness of His infinite presence were
overwhelming, plus the joyful fulfilment of
the Holy Spirit's enveloping assurance that
surrounded every part of my existence was
beyond explanation and only God knows
what I went through. I know I will never
forget that encounter of eternal bliss. The
euphoria—that I knew that I knew—that
I could move onward with the Lord into
eternity was peace beyond explanation
because I knew without doubt that I was
and am the righteousness of God in Christ.
2Cor. 5:21 **God made Him who knew no
sin to be sin on our behalf, so that in Him
we might become the righteousness of
God**.

I was aware of the inability to think of sin or anything outside of purity. The white light of the Lord's love and presence did not allow anything other than who God is to be evident in that space and time. Jesus is Lord and how true that every knee will bow to Him. I felt like I could step forward into my eternity and the knowing I could go filled my heart with anticipation when suddenly, through the whole timeless and jubilant experience I heard my wife praying for me. I felt the loneliness she would be going through if I went on and I could see her struggling with the unknown of what to do next. I said, "Oh Lord, I sure want to go and be with You, but my wife is going to hate all the paperwork that will need to be done, so please have mercy and get me through this." (I know, what can I Do? I'm a firstborn, and we firstborns take care of business before we go on to the next thing.) There was a rush of odd thoughts, but I started to come back to a form of normality, but shook-up. I remembered a quote I had read that morning, "We are never taller than when we are on our knees praying to God." My tongue still felt like a dentist had frozen it, but my thinking was clear. That became a new fear, my thinking was right but my arm and eyes were doing what they wanted without my control. Prov. 3:25 **Be not afraid of sudden fear, neither of the desolation of the wicked, when it comes. 26 For the LORD shall be thy confidence and shall keep thy foot from being taken**. Then suddenly it began to subside.

My wife had called an ambulance. The whole two waves of attack were only a few minutes or so in time, but what a few minutes in time that was. The milliseconds seemed to stretch into long coherent discussions of thoughts, words and actions. By the time my wife was talking to the dispatcher, I was sitting in a chair and she was asking me the questions the 911 medic was asking. "Smile," she said, and then she responded, "Yes, his face and smile are even." "Raise your arms up high," she said. "Yes, his arms are even," and so on it went. The ambulance came and to the hospital, I went. After five hours at the hospital and enduring every type of test, nothing was found to be wrong with me that evening. It was days later that the problem would be discovered.

There are a few lessons that I took away from that scary evening. What was important on August 2nd was no longer important on August 3rd. Priorities had drastically changed. I realized the fear of death had diminished greatly because I know that I know God loves me and will welcome me home when that day comes. It is today that counts, so don't waste it on the offenses or guilt that you are carrying. Psalm 118:24 **This is the day which the LORD hath made; we will rejoice and be glad in it**. I realized that we will not be able to bring any of that old self-centered stuff with us, so we may as well leave it here today. Forgive everyone and everything you have to forgive. Let go of all the guilt your martyred complex is hanging on to, and enter into the joy of the Lord because that is worth having. Another thing that now blesses me is knowing the importance of a clean and clear conscience. That was such a comfort during that frightful event, and yet peace eventually prevailed because of knowing the Prince of Peace who also knows me. 1John 5:14 **And this is the confidence that we have in him, that, if we ask anything according to his will, he hears us:** 15 **And if we know that he hear us, whatsoever we ask, we know that we have the petitions that we desired of him**. Live with no regrets. Hug your children, call your parents and tell them you love them. Smile and kiss your spouse because in a millisecond it can be all over, and oh ya, start getting the paperwork in order.

The Disease

After returning home from the hospital, I knew I was responsible for the bad health I was in. It was my bad eating habits and my stressed overworked lifestyle that brought about the sickness that caused my heart to flutter, miss a beat, and tire very easily. The state of my health condition was my fault and not the fault of the government, food industry, pharmaceutical practices or the condition of our society. Yes, there are contributing factors from these governing and business entities and the society we live in, but the final decision to accept their offerings of junk foods, lazy routines and medical bias was still my choice. I caused the heart disease that I was suffering from and I repented to God for the way I had treated His temple of the Holy Spirit. 1Cor. 6:19 **Do you not know that your bodies are temples of the Holy Spirit, who is in you, whom you have received from God? You are not your own;** 20 **you were bought at a price. Therefore honor God with your bodies.**

It was days later during that eventful week that the diagnosis I received revealed I had Atrial fibrillation and my heart was missing a beat. The scans revealed that during the millisecond of missing the said beat, a clot had formed and made its way to my brain, causing the stroke. This simple explanation is a scary thought to live with, as the idea of having a heart that is missing a beat here and there was unsettling.

The worst part of the whole ordeal was the realization that I was an obese man who had become, through my own choices, 260 pounds or about 90 pounds overweight and working out was going to be a hard row to hoe. I started walking every day. Sometimes it was the road behind my house that was an uphill walk and other times it was the flat areas in the park. Many times I had to sit on the curb to get my breath and go through the full feeling of a fibrillation attack that rendered my walking difficult to keep going.

The effects of Afib on my body were terrible because I was also dealing with the lingering effects of the stroke at the same time. I could not handle major noises. Something as simple as driving with the window down, the sound of the oncoming traffic was bouncing all over my mind and I could not get stabilized or oriented as there was a constant echo. Loud noises would cause frightful stress and I would have to pull over and rest till the spell was done. If I dropped a plate or something at the table, I would feel overwhelmed as if I was going to be in trouble for breaking a cup or glass. The anxiety was palpable and the emotions were all over the place. The feeling that my mind was just outside of my head about four inches to the top right was freaking me out because I felt like I was trying to catch up to it in a similar way to the carrot in front of the donkey pulling the cart.

There is a side effect that happens to patients who suffer strokes and heart attacks that no one warns you about. I was fortunate to have an uncle who had gone through by-pass operations and other complications and he had warned me that mood swings and the feeling of blues would take over for long periods. The feelings of anxiety and wanting to cry would come upon me at different times of the day but especially after messing something up. Whether it is at home, work, or sitting in a restaurant after dropping a fork or napkin on the floor, there would be a rush of anxious sadness hitting me and I couldn't figure out why dropping a fork was such a terrible mistake. We all know it isn't a mistake or even a problem, but for some reason, my emotions would rise within and become very accusatory as if I had just pushed the nuclear button that will start the next world war, and it is all my fault. Not only was I feeling my way through the physical problems the Afib was causing, but all the extras that came along with that disease were like a plague that would not stop. I read up on this blues mood swing attack and apparently, this can keep happening for up to three years after the traumas that take place in a person's heart and brain because of the stroke and heart attack's reaction in a physical body.

This uneasy feeling and undesirable reaction that was accompanying the drug that was not working for me was taking place in my mind, and it was messing with my ability to stand in a balanced position without toppling over. I sauntered, trying to walk a straight line because I kept drifting to the right as I chased and looked for the normal feeling of a clear head. My wife said she could tell when an attack/ spell was coming on because my bottom lip would lose its colour and I would get that thousand-yard stare in my eyes. I would need to lay down till the spell was over. This would happen a few times a day, and sometimes more.

The Sick Health Care System

There is no doubt that our medical system looks like a Dr. Seuss picture book of a structure that is held up and braced by crooked sticks and broken boxes. A person has no idea how much dysfunction is going on until you are a number and someone being processed through the workings of the healthcare system. After a few rounds of going here and there and not getting any real answers, a kind of frustrated loss of hope starts to work its way into a person's soul.

While I was fighting to get my heart and

life back, I was also fighting the medical system which (for me) had no real answers as to how to heal my heart. They had a long list of tests that led to more tests, and multiple prescriptions that when looked into, the side effects were worse than the fibrillation attacks. I felt trapped because those in the health system kept pointing out all the terrible things that MIGHT happen to me if I did not take the five prescriptions being pushed on me at the time. One of the arguments I got into with one of the doctors was over the beta blockers they wanted me to take. I asked them why they would want to slow my heart down if it was already missing a beat and the fact that my heart rate was not high in any way did not make their advice seem like good medical sense. The abrupt answer I got was, "This is the only menu we have and you need to get on board with the program!" I said, "Your menu is wrong if it is prescribing synthetic medication for something I do not have. Why would you prescribe the same thing for each individual person with different medical issues? Should we not be diagnosed on a case-by-case basis if we have different problems?" Again the doctor said, "It's the only menu we have!" Then the doctor left the room. The other doctor in the room was an Atrial fibrillation doctor, and she said there was no cure, so I had better get used to the medications being offered and that one day there might be some advancements that would bring healing. As I left for home and headed to my car in the hospital parking lot, I sent up a flare prayer asking God to show me what to do. Then I vowed to do my own studying to heal my heart that I had messed up.

I got home in time for the noon news and there was a piece on some Swedish doctors who were having great success healing Atrial fibrillation. I googled the 2012 articles the doctors had published along with notes on their research that were available to download. The next day, I brought what I had and located the doctors who the day before said there was no cure. I gave them the information and they said, "The Canadian medical system does not recognize this work yet, because we have not done our own tests." I asked if they could use me as the guinea pig for the tests in Canada because I was a perfect candidate since I did not smoke or drink alcohol. They poo-pooed that idea too. Why was no one in the system looking for a healthy, natural, and successful way of healing the public, plus trying to find a way to correct the beat of my heart? And why were prescription drugs so much on the top of the list of what they would offer?

Over the next few months, I went through test after test and doctor's appointment after appointment and all I can say is that finding a way to get healed was not on anyone's agenda. Just more prescriptions and more tests were recommended. I woke up one morning with a buzzing feeling in my knees, hands, and cheekbones. I walked into cardiology and described everything and pointed out that I thought I was being poisoned by the blood thinner that had been given as a prescription. My cardiologist was not in that day, and the one on call made a mockery of the symptoms I was having. He said that it was all in my head. My cardiologist's assistant happened to be in the room when he said this, and the look of astonishment on her face told me this doctor had crossed some type of ethical line. One hour later, that wonderful assistant came out and said, "You are right Mr. Sawyer, these pills are harming your body and mind."

One of the major cautions that comes with some of these new drugs are the warning that suicidal thoughts may happen and of course, you are to check in with your doctor so that they can prescribe something else. The frightening thing that started to happen while I was on this particular blood thinner were not suicidal thoughts, but rather, I started agreeing with dying. I was saying things like, "Lord, if I could see my sons before I die, I could give them all the passwords to everything and I can say goodbye properly." My wife was out of the country dealing with her ailing parents and I would say, "Lord it would be nice if I could see my wife before I go so I can help her with all the paperwork that will happen when I die. Help me stay alive until she comes home." I was not suicidal at all; I was being affected by the medication, and the enemy of my soul was taking advantage of the weakness I was going through. The devil was lying to me saying I was alone and being abandoned. Deep down I knew that was a lie because the Word of God says He will never leave us nor forsake us. Heb. 13:5b **For God has said, "I will never fail you. I will never abandon you."**

Finally, something to smile about. For the first time in a long time, the medical practitioners agreed with me and listened to me. They finally saw that I was being severely affected by the prescription. Then the bombshell of bombshells came out of the assistant's mouth. She said, "Well this is good that this has happened to you, we can now prescribe what we know works rather than what we have been told to prescribe." Verbatim were her words, and these words were bouncing off my tottering mind. The hair on the back of my neck went up as I realized they had been pushing whatever the head of the department had said must be pushed as a blood thinner.

Within two hours of taking the new blood thinner, I got my balance back, my mind was back in my head rather than on the side of it, and the people in the office kept commenting that the colour in my face was back and I was walking normally again. By mid-day, I was capable of reasoning and dealing with complex problems at work. I felt good for the first time in months. We often do not know how bad we had it until the cloud of despair leaves us clear-minded and ready to fight the next issue.

I came home and vowed to God that I would no longer cooperate with the hospital system as I could not trust BIG Medical and from now on, I was going to take my health into my own hands. If I succeeded fine, and If I failed fine, it was my line in the sand. I said, "God, either heal me or take me home! I am done with the health SCARE system." I said, "Father, there are about eight billion people on Earth, and You know every one of them. I need to meet the person who knows how to heal my heart. Can you arrange that meeting for me?"

A few days later I arrived at church and a married couple I knew well were coming into the church at the same time from the other end of the lobby. They both saw me at the same time and were frantically pointing their fingers at me. They rushed up to me and said at the same time, "God put you on our heart this morning individually and we mentioned this to each other on the way down here and we both had the same message for you. You are to read a book called Diet Evolution!" They went on to explain that they did not know why that book in particular because the doctor who wrote it believed in evolution and other disclaimers, when I interrupted and said, "This is my answer I prayed about. I asked God to let me meet the person, doctor, or whoever knows how to heal my heart and as far as I am concerned, this book is the first step where I will get some answers. Thank you so much for obeying the Spirit of the Lord, and loving me enough to give me your prayer's attention."

I bought the book and started applying everything I was learning because I had the confidence that God had led me to find some of the tools I would need to begin my healing journey. Around the same time, I reasoned that I would continue to see my regular doctor who was very knowledgeable concerning Afib as this was his field of practice before he became a family doctor. He asked me to do one more test to clear up his notes and if I still wanted to drop all the medical advice and appointments that were set up for me then he would work with me because he could see that I was serious and was going to fight this disease with or without them. He also asked me to stay in touch with my cardiologist because he too could see I was already doing things that would improve my health and he wanted to work with me on my terms. Praise the Lord, the healing journey was afoot.

Discipline With Prescriptions

One of the hardest and intimidating times of recovery is when all the prescription drugs are recommended. I had blown out arguments with a few of the doctors in the BC Health CARE system. I was labelled an uncooperative patient because they had five prescriptions for me the week of my stroke. I explained to them that four of the prescriptions could be taken away if I just changed the way I lived by only eating real food and exercising. These actions would take care of the overweight issues and I only needed a blood thinner until I figured out how to replace that. I had a bit of a delay in my step after the stroke when I walked. I noticed it for a few months but I got through that by walking every day until I had lost 60 pounds and the delay was gone. Then I started going to the gym regularly and did some intense CrossFit training until I lost another 32 pounds. At that time I was sixty-three years old and I could feel the difference that was taking place in my health. The results motivated me to become more disciplined to the point I was doing some kind of exercise every day of the week. Saturdays and Sundays were my rest days, so I walked a small three-kilometre circuit around a nearby park.

The doctors worked with me when they saw the results I was achieving and they noticed that my damaged heart was healing in an odd way. They could not figure out how my heart had found a rhythm within the miss-rhythm and that I had very good blood pressure. Some of the cardiologists from Western Canada repeatedly asked the question, "How is it possible that he has good blood pressure when his heart is missing a beat?" My doctor said that for some reason my heart craved hard work. Therefore, I figured first thing early every morning I would give my heart what it wanted. It wanted major labour, so I gave it some at the gym.

There had been a plan to go through a procedure called a cardiac ablation when I turned seventy years old, but the cardiologist said they would not do the ablation because my heart was still getting better even though it still missed a beat. They did not want to go in and disturb the healing I was causing. I had a hard time with that explanation but reasoned that God was still doing a healing work to my heart. Isa. 57:18 **I have seen his ways, and healed him, and comforted him, and given him true comfort**. I had to remain disciplined in my workout program, as well as my anti-inflammatory eating regimen which helped me prove I did not need the beta blockers, statins and other prescribed stuff they were pressuring me to take. For all the fight and discipline I have worked through, there is something that needs to be taken into consideration. All the workouts, eating habits, and diligence I have put forth towards my health does not mean I will live any longer in years, because I caused the original damage to my heart through my terrible lifestyle choices. But hopefully, it means I will have quality of life while I am here.

Other Thoughts

Proverbs 4:22 For they are life unto those that find them, and health to all their flesh.

We have all thought the same after we have seen and heard the countless amounts of commercials that say, "Ask your doctor if this toxic drug is for you" (paraphrased). How would anyone on earth have time for all the appointments it would take to ask your doctor about the healing claims and side effect warnings of all the synthetic drugs that are offered to heal a natural body? On top of that, does the doctor even know all the reams of information on all the synthetic snake oil treatments offered? If I were a doctor I would cringe every time I heard another commercial directing the fear-filled public to make an appointment to "ask your doctor." We have all heard the term looking for love in all the wrong places; well, the same public is looking for peace and well-being in all the wrong places also. 2Tim. 3:7 **Ever learning, and never able to come to the knowledge of the truth**.

As strange as this sounds, one of the questions I now ask a person when depression is the reason for a consultation is, "What medications are you on?" You have heard the expression Prozac Nation; that comes from the book title. Well, it is not just an expression. It is mainstream and yes, even in the church. Most of the time the story is the same. The person was feeling depressed and the doctor prescribed an antidepressant and it worked great for a day or two, then it went downhill from there on and the depression was still in full aggression to a point of desperation. Now, feeling sick and overwhelmed with a heavy heart and still depressed, they are seeking any kind of help for healing. Another one of those vicious circles that some people fall into.

The Lord Jesus has been described as the great physician and healer of all who come to him. Jesus healed every type of disease and malady that ever was and is. This blessed healing is still available to us all when we ask by faith. John 14:12 **I tell you the truth, anyone who believes in me will do the same works I have done, and even greater works, because I am going to be with the Father**. Thank you, Lord, that there is healing for us, even in this skeptical and unbelieving time in our nation. Psalm 107:20 **He sent his Word, and healed them, and delivered them from their destructions**. If you are going to take the time to ask your doctor for some help, then take the same time and ask your Lord for healing or at least wisdom for the doctor who will give you the right health care.

I think of the poor woman who had suffered a great deal under the care of many doctors and spent all that she had on trying to get healed for twelve years. This sounds like a typical North American medical story gone bad, but it was another healing that Jesus gave to an everyday ordinary person just like you and me. Mark 5:25 **And a certain woman, which had an issue of blood twelve years, 26 And had suffered many things of many physicians, and had spent all that she had, and was nothing bettered, but rather grew worse**. The more things change, the more they stay the same. She had a medical problem for twelve years. Many doctors gave prescriptions and practiced medicine on her to the point where she went broke and her condition grew worse. At this point, her medical insurance would not cover what she needed because of big pharma. Oh well, you get the picture. The good news is that Jesus healed her. Mark 5:34 **And he said to her, "Daughter, your faith has made you well. Go in peace. Your suffering is over**. Like this woman, many of us will come to the point of desperation before we reach out and touch the hem of the Lord's garment per se, or reach for the healing power of Jesus Christ by faith. Mark 5:28 **For she said, If I may touch but his clothes, I shall be whole**. The Master Physician lives in our hearts and His anointed healing power also resides there.

Ask Doctor Jesus for the cure to all your ailments. Talking with God is the better place to start because you might get wisdom from God as to what you should change in your lifestyle, diet, or devotion that will heal you. This was my experience when the Lord helped me find healing. 3John 1:2 **Beloved, I wish above all things that thou may prosper and be in health, even as thy soul prospers**. Don't forget your Lord in all your searching for healing of all the ailments in your life. Stay on message with your God and do the things that will heal you, but most importantly also do the things that will keep you well after the healing has come to full fruition. Psalm 103:2 **Bless the LORD, O my soul, and forget not all his benefits: 3 Who forgives all thine iniquities; who heals all thy diseases**.

Other Thoughts

Proverbs 17:22 A joyful heart is good medicine, but a broken spirit drains one's strength.

What Does Removing Stress In My Life Look Like? The dictionary describes stress happening to a person as "a state of mental or emotional strain or tension resulting from adverse or very demanding circumstances."

We have come to know that stress is a lot more damaging to the health of the human body, soul, and mind than previously thought. Stress is responsible for countless deadly ailments people are struggling with today worldwide. Stressfulness in society is affecting people's ability to sleep, digest foods, work efficiently, be at peace, and even get along with their neighbours. Things seem to be at the point of snapping when any extra stress comes along to weigh down the mind more than it already is. Every little thing can be blown up into a stressful situation because peace is eluding so many people. Psalm 2:1 **Why are the nations so angry? Why do they waste their time with futile plans?**

Stress was one of the main factors that caused the stroke I had experienced. The doctor said, "You will have to get rid of stress in your life." I said, "Really? What does that look like in my life?" The doctor was reading from a general menu of platitudes and suggestions for helping their patients; therefore, my question caught her off guard. She looked at me questioningly and I said again, "What does a stress-free life look like for me in my life? How do I go about getting rid of it?" I went on to say, "Look at yourself. You have a small twitch under your eye and your left hand has a small tremor and you look overworked and your breathing is shallow and you look fatigued. Shouldn't you be following your own advice?" She said, "Oh Norm, why do you always have to turn this thing around? Why can't you just take the medicine?" She began to laugh and I joined in the laughter because that was true medicine. Prov. 17:22a **A joyful heart is good medicine**.

One of the natural prescriptions I found for a stress-free life is found in 1Thes. 5:18 **Give thanks in every circumstance, for this is God's will for you in Christ Jesus**. Gratefulness and thankfulness is a whole-life medicine that helps the entire body, soul, and spirit stay healed. Another thing I have tried to do is see the word stress as an acronym. 'Stop Treating Regular Events So Seriously.' Stop the madness so to speak. Take joy in the day we are in and be grateful for that day as tomorrow is not promised to any of us. Psalm 118:24 **This is the day that the LORD has made; let us rejoice and be glad in it**.

Every generation has had to deal with stressful events. Whether it was the invading

Vikings, Barbarian hordes, church atrocities and inquisitions, Spanish invaders, Nazi cruelties or fanatical Islamic insanity—there has been stress throughout world history. Eccl. 3:8 **A time to love, and a time to hate; a time of war, and a time of peace.** Everyone throughout time has had to learn how to de-stress or fall to the consequences of a life of debilitating stressed-out fear.

God asks us to trust in Him for the peace that will eradicate stress in our lives. He admonishes us to look to Him and look for Him in a meaningful way. Jer. 29:18 **You will seek me and find me when you seek me with all your heart.** The Lord directs us to keep our eyes looking heavenward, focused on the solution and expectation of receiving from Him the answers to overcoming stress. Psalm 121:1 **I lift up my eyes to the hills. From where does my help come? 2 My help comes from the LORD, Who made heaven and earth.** Stress is a tool of the enemy of our soul. If the devil can get us focused on the problems in life, then stress will build up. This is the medicine I have prescribed for myself and this prescription can be shared.

Stop treating regular events so seriously and start giving thanks to God in all things. With His grace actively working in our lives, we will find the solutions we are looking for. Matt. 11:28 **Then Jesus said, "Come to me, all of you who are weary and carry heavy burdens, and I will give you rest**.

When I cannot get answers to life's problems, I ask God to show me how to overcome them and what steps to take. After the last appointment with the cardiologist, I asked God "What does removing stress in my life look like?" At 2:00 am I woke up with the vision of the word STRESS in a linear line as an acronym. I could see the sign and words Stop Treating Regular Events So Seriously. Then I heard in my spirit, "This is what a stress-free life looks like for you." The next morning I got the opportunity to apply this new revelation in my life. As I was on my way to work, suddenly I saw a pressure gauge on my dashboard drop while the smell of antifreeze entered the car and the hiss of steam coming out the hood of the car. I was fortunate to be two blocks from my mechanic's shop and drove clunking away to the shop. When I pulled into the parking lot and stopped there was a green puddle forming under the radiator and my friend and mechanic Rick came out and said, "You look calm for a mess like this." I said, "Rick, I've been on the road for about fifty years, car repairs are a regular event, so let's just get this fixed. Can I use a loaner car till it is done so I can go to work?" Rick laughed and said "I can get a new water pump in this today, see you later." There it was, the beginning of discerning how to react to regular events. No stress was needed. Car repairs are regular events, no point stressing over it.

What does a stress-free life look like for you? This is the crux of our lives and we all need to find what it is that affects us in particular. Once we find the trigger to stress that makes us ill, then it is time to apply the discipline it takes to become healed and walk in that freedom.

Jim Rohn said, "One discipline always leads to another discipline."

Part Five

Discipline In Eating

The biggest change that had to happen was in the foods that I was consuming at an unhealthy rate. There should be a different category for real food versus processed products made with processed ingredients. To call all the chemical powders and additives that are packaged in convenient boxes and labelled nutritious, natural, and healthy should have another word to describe it than food. Maybe *Stuff In A Box* and big bright labels that say "May Cause Death" would be a good place to start. The observation is true when walking through a grocery store. The real food is on the outer edges of the store and the processed products are on the middle shelves. Stay away from the middle for a few months and see your life change. I had to concentrate on the healing of my heart and choose foods that would help heal my heart because that was the issue and the reason for the stroke happening in the first place. My heart was missing a beat here and there and a clot formed and made its way to my brain.

The food choices had to become a stubborn activity on my part, and I was fortunate to know how to cook. This kept the peace in the kitchen and with my wife's choices of what she wanted to eat. I was the one who needed healing and there was no need to make my wife get on my health program because she was already making healthy choices. This is one of the areas that are difficult for the spouse who does not have a gluttonous eating problem. When the poor other spouses start changing things and trying to help with food choices, it often causes unwanted arguments and no one is feeling good about healthy life choices. If you are a male and have become obese and sick through your bad eating habits, then at least have the courtesy to get off your lazy boy chair and learn how to cook so that you can heal yourself.

The number of times women have asked my wife, "How did you get Norm to change his lifestyle choices and eating habits and stay on his exercise routine?" My wife calmly says, "I can't get Norm to do anything. He did it all on his own, and I am proud of him." This is the rub. Men, you need to stop using your wife's cooking as an excuse for your inability to step away from the table. Gluttony is a personal sin and must be dealt with in prayer, repentance and the discipline to step away from the table. Prov. 23:2 **And put a knife to thy throat, if thou be a man given to appetite**.

After going through all the pantry items and looking for words on the packaged products that I could not pronounce, I chucked them all out into the rubbish where most of it belongs. I started buying grass-fed meats and organic vegetables, plus resisting all the sweet products that are available wherever we go throughout our daily lives. I did not know how many donuts, candy and sweet treats there were available for the picking until I started removing these items from my life. The art of finding all the healthy foods became a quest of sorts since there were not many stores offering these products at the time. I had to go to all the farmer's markets, order specialty items and pay the extra costs (did I mention that eating healthy was an inconvenience). I am happy to say that in the valley where I live, there are many options for very healthy foods of all kinds. It seems the trend is catching on in this area.

Another discipline that I acted upon was to try and find foods that were within two degrees of knowing where the foods came from. Zero degrees is that I am growing the food and know the quality of its growth and origin. One degrees is knowing the farmer who grows the products and raises the animals and how the animals are treated. I do not know why this became important to me that the animals were treated as humanely as possible but it was a side issue that showed up when I was choosing the products I would buy. Prov. 12:19 **A righteous man regardeth the life of his beast: but the tender mercies of the wicked are cruel**. Two degrees is dealing with the distributor who knows the farmer and the healthy practices they are using to bring healthy products to the public. After that, we do not know how and where the food comes from. Even if the sign in the local grocer says, "Locally grown." Who knows what the locals are doing to get their products into major grocery stores?

All of these new lifestyle changes started to add up and I could see the results were good. I could walk faster and farther. I could lift heavier weights and work out longer. I could work around the yard without waves of fatigue washing over me. I did feel younger in heart and spirit. The reality was that the time it took to get up early and work out plus the extra effort that had to be made while preparing and making real food choices was the price I had to pay for a better life if I did not want to live in a state of pain and sickness in my later years.

An important sidebar here is that I am not a nutritionist, but no matter how perfect your food choices are, you may need to continue to make changes as you get older. Over the last decade, I have had to tweak the consumption of certain foods even though the food is real, organic, and good for the body. In my case recently I have had to deal with muscle pain that showed up one day.

I found out I had too much protein in my diet. I know that protein is sacrosanct to many health enthusiasts but it does not work for me at this time and I removed some of the high-protein foods for now. Yes, it did not take long until my muscles felt better and the pain was gone. Therefore, there is not just one thing that will heal the whole mess you might be going through. It will be a combination of different wholesome foods, activities, and choices that will bring better health overall.

Another food I had to cut back on is the trusty apple. Over the years the genetic changes being made to apples are now affecting me. Those who genetically modify fruits and vegetables have increased the sugar content in apples to levels that do not sit well with me. I have had to find heirloom apple trees from years gone by that have not been messed with. I am fortunate to have two heirloom apple trees that have normal sucrose levels in the fruit, but how many people have these trees within their reach? This is our future. We will need to know what is being added genetically to foods.

The apples, bananas, strawberries, papaya and tomatoes are no longer what they once were. Ask God where to find foods that work in your body and also bring nutritious health as well. Did I mention that preparing and being responsible for good food was inconvenient?

I'll tell you what is more inconvenient—being schlepped around to numerous doctor's appointments by people and family who tolerate the task of getting your sick body to the doctor's appointment on time. Needing help to put some heavy stuff away on a top shelf. Not being able to go where and when you want because your body is inflamed all the time because of the junk food you insist on eating. The so-called convenience of the modern-day diet is stealing your future convenience of living relatively agile and healthy. The choice is yours and always has been. Deut. 30:19 **Today I have given you the choice between life and death, between blessings and curses. Now I call on heaven and earth to witness the choice you make. Oh, that you would choose**

life so that you and your descendants might live! The message is, "Oh that you would make some right choices and live."

The discipline it took for me in the area of food choices was one of the hardest battles I had to fight through to regain my health when I was sick, obese, and disillusioned with all the experts. I had to take responsibility for what I was eating and the quantity of food eaten. I had to look up, research the best I could, and discern all the true and false information that was available, and decide how I was going to get back on the right side of living. It was up to me to pray, research, and learn to cook with nutritional foods. It was not my wife's problem nor anyone's fault but my own fault for the unhealthy state I created when the stroke occurred. The discipline became easier when I stopped lying to myself and saying things like, "Well this piece of cake should be okay, or this extra deep fried blah blah blah will be fine for this time." This Chinese proverb was what I needed to take note of, *"The man who blames others has a long way in his journey to go. The man who blames himself is halfway there. The man who blames no one has already arrived.*" God has a simpler way of saying what the Chinese proverb says. Prov. 23:2 **And put a knife to thy throat, If thou be a man given to appetite**. That was it, I stopped blaming everything out there and became disciplined in fixing and choosing what I knew to be clean healthy foods that would conquer the voracious appetite that needed taming. With the help of the Holy Spirit day by day I got better at saying "NO THANK YOU!" to all processed carbs, treats, and sweets that my fat cells once screamed for. The shift in appetite changed to wanting to eat and cook with real food. Praise the Lord for that victory. Col. 3:17 **And whatever you do, whether in word or deed, do it all in the name of the Lord Jesus, giving thanks to God the Father through Him**.

It will take effort and discipline for anyone who emphatically desires to turn their health around. As many of my contemporaries and I enter our elderly years, hopefully we will be able to do it in relative health so that we may continue to follow the call the Lord has placed upon our lives. I want to be ministering what the Lord has placed upon my heart and not spending time shopping for a walker or sitting in doctor's waiting rooms wishing I had made better health choices. I want to be the man the Psalmist says will bear fruit in old age and I want to be spry when I do it. Psalm 92:13 **They are planted in the house of the LORD; they flourish in the courts of our God.** 14 **They still bear fruit in old age; they are ever full of sap and green,** 15 **to declare that the LORD is upright; he is my rock, and there is no unrighteousness in Him**. Yes, this is what I want to do in old age. I want to finish the race God has set before me, and I want to cross the finish line on my own two feet, arm and arm with my Lord and Saviour, Jesus Christ while hearing, "Well done, Norm!"

Other Thoughts

Proverbs 23:2 And put a knife to thy throat, if thou be a man given to appetite.

At the time when I got serious about living and covenanted with myself that I would become disciplined in how and what I would eat, I started reading the book that was recommended to me by my friends from the church assembly we attend. The results were noticeable in a short time. There were immediate changes that started to take place as I applied the principles and methods to a lifestyle change. You cannot pretend to be disciplined in how and what you eat, because in a short time your eating habits will show up on and in your body. I once heard a Weight Watcher member repeat a slogan from that organization. "What you eat in private shows in public." There it is in simplicity. In other words, your gluttony will find you out. It is interesting that when I meet someone going through a bad health experience, they always seem to know deep down that they need to change their eating habits and get on an exercise program. The confusion is normally which of the thousands of diets and routines they should get onto.

We need to realize that it is not a diet that one must become disciplined in, it is a lifestyle change that will most likely need to be paid attention to and tweaked now and then when there are reactions in the body because of the considerable changes taking place. Diets are normally a trend that does not last for more than two months, and once the results of fitting into that new dress or sports coat are achieved, then back to the junk food that the body is screaming for because it has been deprived for a time and the carbs are taking over your willingness to remain disciplined. A lifestyle change is a different choice altogether. The choice to remain true to yourself and in most cases to our God who we also made some promises to—that if He got us through the hard days of sickness we would change our ways. This lifestyle choice will have times of regimented self-talk and proclamations of what our intentions were when we first decided to live rather than exist in the infirmities of life.

We need to answer the question of real food versus commercial ingredients. What is it going to be? The preparation of real food is an inconvenience but a necessary discipline if you are going to learn how to eat quality foods that will heal your body and give it the endurance it needs to handle life's challenges. The health of our whole body, soul and spirit should be the goal of our life.

Other Thoughts

Proverbs 11:1 The LORD detests the use of dishonest scales, but he delights in accurate weights.

The above Proverb says it plainly, "The Lord hates cheating and delights in honesty." A noncommittal attitude with no honest effort given to overcoming bad habits and strongholds in our life will not work. As a matter of fact, in most cases, the problem will get deeply entrenched and become harder to overcome because of the lazy spirit within the one who is in bondage. A sluggard learns to live with the personal prison that was made by his own attitude. Prov. 21:25 **The desire of the sluggard kills him, for his hands refuse to labor**.

"What is your cheat day? How many times a week do you get to cheat on your health system?" I have been asked these questions so many times over the last five years because of the large amount of weight I have lost and kept it off. My answer is, "I lost all the weight by the grace of God. The strength God gave me to stay with the program He laid out for me did not include cheat days." To regain my health, I had to stop cheating when it came to a lack of exercise and eating certain foods. There were no more gluttonous cheat days. It was my previous lifestyle of cheating that caused the illness in the first place. It was a lifestyle change God led me through and not another fad diet. I needed self-control in my life. If your first question is, "What is your cheat day?" then whatever you want to overcome will not get done. Your focus is on cheating and not conquering. God detests cheating and that includes when you cheat yourself. Why would God participate in helping you cheat yourself out of the blessings of God? John 10:10b **I am come that they might have life, and that they might have it more abundantly**. There is the ridiculousness of our times—wanting to start a new life emphasizing a cheat day. It is like saying, "Okay Lord, now that you saved my soul, when can I return to sinning? Once or twice a week would be nice. What do you think Lord? Does that work for you?" You would not say that to God, yet you do say it to yourself when overcoming hard things in your life. You are either in it to win it, or not at all. We are no longer children befuddled by all the sparkles and glitter. 1Cor. 13:11 **When I was a child, I spake as a child, I understood as a child, I thought as a child: but when I became**

a man, I put away childish things.

This has become my cheat. I cheat the enemy of my soul by praying for the lost souls God puts on my heart. I cheat the devil by believing and praying by faith for the healing of those who are sick and suffering a disease. I cheat the spirits of darkness by submitting to God and repenting when I sin. James 4:7 **Submit yourselves therefore to God. Resist the devil, and he will flee from you**. If you want a cheat day, then cheat the enemy out of having control in your life. Satan has been cheating the saints of God for centuries out of the blessings that are truly theirs. Don't cheat yourself out of the blessings of God. Get rid of the dishonest scales you have been using to justify a cheating and shallow lifestyle. Start using the honest and accurate scales God has given you through grace to live within the blessings of God. After all, they are our blessings. Prov. 11:1 **The LORD detests the use of dishonest scales, but he delights in accurate weights**. God delights in your prosperity and overcomer attitude that is lived through Christ. By grace, say it and mean it! "No more cheat days!"

Norm Sawyer said: "Motivation will get you to the gym, but discipline keeps you going regularly."

Discipline In Exercise

We all know we need to exercise. We know deep down in our souls we need to train our bodies to work out and remain as healthy as possible. However, the circumstances of life give us permission to be slack, lazy, and invent excuses for not taking care of our bodies. The numerous excesses are at the tip of our tongues the moment we think there will be pain or inconvenience. We simply do not want to put in the effort because laziness and convenience have become our default settings. This was my problem until I was forced to tear down, rip away, and blow up every excuse that presented itself to my ailing body. My choice was live, or die a slow decrepit death of wasting away into old age. This is not what I wanted nor what I feel God wants for us. The Lord declares that we will bear fruit in old age. Psalm 92:14 **In old age they will still bear fruit; healthy and green they will remain**. How can I bear healthiness in old age if I do not put in the effort?

The Covenant

After the stroke, and the realization that it was going to be a long way back to a semblance of health, I needed to be accountable to God and myself for the mess I had made of my heart and my health. The only thing I could do was to first admit I was obese and that it was my fault I had caused the fibrillation my heart was experiencing. You cannot fix what you do not acknowledge needs fixing. I needed to change my lifestyle entirely and not fall for some pseudo Readers Digest cute—a few days a week, five minutes a day— exercise program that is forgotten about two weeks after promising oneself they are serious about getting into shape. Oh please, enough of the lying to myself. It was going to take a lifestyle change of the greatest extreme measures that I had ever done.

I made a covenant with the Lord by first admitting I had been wrong in the choices I had made toward my health. There was not an exact understanding of what percentage of the heart use I had left but I said, "Lord, if my heart is only working at 70% of its capacity, then you can count on the fact that from now on I will give you 100% of that 70. I will believe by faith for a new heart or that you will heal the one I have, but I give what I have left to you to train me in the way of healing." This agreement proved to be the right strategy because from that time on I stuck to the program and the dietary needs to do the exercise and workouts that would be required to come back from the mess I had created of my health. I started walking every day for two years and added going to the gym four days a week and the results were paying off. I then changed the workout routines every three months, so that my body did not become used to the same workouts. Today, I still change my exercise routines about every four months and I am on the gym floor by 5:00 AM five days a week. I walk a few kilometres two days a week which I consider my rest time. Ten years have passed since the stroke and I have kept the ninety-two pounds I lost off my frame and have continued to tweak my daily workouts to help my aging body adapt to more training so that I can stay as healthy as possible. Yes, I wish I had the jam of character to have committed myself to healthy choices when I was in my forties, but that is only wishful thinking. I can do what I can do now to be the best version of myself at this time.

It may be that you will need to make a covenant with God to get through your hard times. I can assure you that the Lord will keep His end of the bargain you present. Only you can mess it up with more lies, excuses, and apathy. Remember, if you lie to me, you are a liar, but if you lie to yourself, then you are a fool. How do you want to play it? It's your choice, it has always been your choice. Hopefully, you want to be a disciplined person of integrity and follow through on your commitment to excellence.

Socrates: No man has the right to be an amateur in the matter of physical training. It is a shame for a man to grow old without seeing the beauty and strength of which his body is capable.

Other Thoughts

Proverbs 25:19 Confidence in an unfaithful man in time of trouble is like a broken tooth, and a foot out of joint.

I saw stars, then tears started to form just after I had stubbed my big toe on a forty-five pound steel plate I had been using to exercise with. The weight did not move, but my toe did as I walked into the solid piece I had just put down on the floor. "Ouch, ouch!" I cried because I could have sworn I heard a crunch when I stubbed my toe dead on center. "Oh Father, Oh God," I said as I limped around. As the pain subsided, I then said, "Listen, Norm, this is not an excuse. Even if you limp, finish your workout!" Even if you limp, don't stop believing God's word for the healing and restoration you need in your life. Even if you are lying flat on your back, keep believing God to help you stand into the fulness of His blessings. While you are hurting, keep believing God for relief and restoration. Even if you limp, keep walking toward God's goodness. Prov. 30:1b **I am weary, God, but I can prevail**.

The key to our victory is to keep our hope and confidence in the character of God who does not lie. Num. 23:19a **God is not a man, that he should lie, nor a human being, that he should change his mind**. The question we have to answer comes down to, who are we going to trust—God or all the varied assumptions that mankind comes up with? Prov. 25:19 **Confidence in an unfaithful man in time of trouble is like a broken tooth, and a foot out of joint**. The world system can only offer a patchwork of substandard help that falls short of God's perfection. Only God can give you the real help you need in the moment of your suffering. Our Lord has all the answers for what we will face in life.

In the Gospel of Luke, we read the story of the ten lepers who stood afar off crying out to Jesus for help. It was while they were in the state of their bacterial flesh-eating sickness that they shuffled and limped their way toward the Lord, looking for mercy. They had been shunned, exiled, and exploited by all people. No one could touch or hug them. They were left to themselves and left to survive on the fringes of the wastelands. As close as the law would allow, they limped their way into the presence of the Lord to get the help they needed. Jesus acknowledges them as redeemable souls and spoke into their lives, with an instruction that would give them hope for their future. Luke 17:14 **When he saw them he said to them, "Go and show yourselves to the priests." And as they went they were cleansed**. As they obeyed, they noticed that their limp was leaving them. The tingling feeling that once ate them alive was now bringing a joyful sensation to their nerve endings. Their act of faith in the Lord's instruction was cleaning up their skin right in front of each other's eyes. Even while they limped, they did as the Lord had said, and healing became their testimony.

Trusting the Lord with all our hearts is the only way we will get victory over the limp that we are suffering from. Prov. 3:5 **Trust in the LORD with all your heart; and lean not unto your own understanding**. It does not matter what the problem is. God can and will help us if we ask by faith. However, we will have to do what the Lord says to overcome the effects the limp has caused. We will need to put our full confidence in the Lord, His Word, and the love He has for us. Even if we limp, we cannot stop believing God. Troubles will come, and battles will happen, but those who trust in the Lord will be saved. Isa. 40:31 **But those who hope in the LORD will renew their strength. They will soar on wings like eagles; they will run and**

not grow weary, they will walk and not be faint. We do not use our limp as an excuse to stop coming to God, we use it to keep seeking God.

Part Six
Discipline In Forgiveness

The gift that forgiveness gives us is freedom within our souls and lives. It frees us from the weight of having to judge everyone's guilt and shame within the paradigm of our flawed reasoning. Forgiving others is not easy to do if we cannot forgive ourselves, or accept the forgiveness God has offered us through His Son Jesus. Many people become bitter in their lives because of something that was unjustly done to them or others. Regardless of the torment the unforgiving person lives in, they seem to steep into the miasma of all that stinks with their lives. The deepest oubliette of their making becomes the prison they live in and make decisions from. The simple instruction that God gives us, "To forgive those who we have something against," is never acted upon and these poor souls wonder in confusion why their prayers seem to vapourize before they reach the heavens. Mark 11:25 **And when you stand praying, if you hold anything against anyone, forgive them, so that your Father in heaven may forgive you your sins**. Before these bound souls can even become disciplined in the act of forgiving, they need to be delivered by God's forgiveness that is available to them through Christ.

Forgiveness is the cornerstone foundation of our faith. Without forgiveness, we would be eternally lost. The purpose of Christ being crucified on the cross was that our sins would be washed away and that we would receive the forgiveness that God had granted us through faith in the Lord's finished redemptive plan. The amazing visual of forgiveness at work was when Jesus looked at the people who were beating Him with whips and nailing Him to the cross, then mocking Him, and He said, "Father, forgive them!" The grace of the Lord was already working toward mankind while Jesus was being crucified. The discipline Jesus exhibited is beyond our understanding, and yet we are forgiven because we accepted Jesus as our Lord and Saviour.

Becoming disciplined in forgiveness will help us become a person who retains the forgiveness of God within one's heart. In the same way, Francis of Assisi asked the Lord to make him an instrument of God's peace, we can ask God to help us become instruments of His forgiveness. We do not 'do' forgiveness, we forgive because it is part of our new nature in Christ. My friend Jami Rogers said, "If we don't understand why God forgives us, then it becomes something to do instead of part of who we are." We are forgiven; therefore, we forgive others. We have all had to forgive the unforgivable at some times in our lives. Those who have gone through this hardship of forgiving, and maintaining their relationship with the Lord have found out that they will need to do it again at some time in their lives. Those who have not continued walking with the Lord after God asked them to forgive the unforgivable have floundered in bitterness only to face a new trauma that keeps them victims of circumstances. This is not where I want to live or be. I need the forgiveness of God working in me so that I have the strength and discipline to forgive those who have sinned against me. God gives us all His strength in this area of our lives.

Other Thoughts

Proverbs 20:20 Whoso curses his father or his mother, his lamp shall be put out in obscure darkness.

Forgiving those who have betrayed or harmed us is hard and even harder is forgiving family members who have done the same. We read of a family betrayal that if it were done today would bring out every type of law enforcement, let alone televise all the emotional scars that would be carved on the person's soul.

Joseph suffered this type of betrayal. Gen. 37:26 **And Judah said unto his brethren,**

What profit is it if we slay our brother, and conceal his blood 27 Come, and let us sell him to the Ishmeelites, and let not our hand be upon him; for he is our brother and our flesh. And his brethren were content. It says, "His brothers were content." This is hardheartedness. To be content with a decision not to murder a brother but rather agree that selling their family member into slavery is a better and more reasonable option? This is all wrong. How did the family become so cold? Yet, after many years Joseph forgives his entire family. Gen. 45:4 **And Joseph said unto his brethren, Come near to me, I pray you. And they came near. And he said, I am Joseph your brother, whom ye sold into Egypt.15 Moreover he kissed all his brethren, and wept upon them: and after that his brethren talked with him**.

My father was a sick and brutal man. I had a horrific childhood but have never used the events of that childhood as an excuse to become a criminal, addicted, or abusive. Were the opportunities available to become an addicted abusive criminal? Yes, but no thanks. Did I struggle with some of the shrapnel that lodged itself in my soul? Yes, but with time and the grace of my Lord Jesus, I was delivered from its pain and crushing weight through the forgiving of my father. In 1996 I wrote the story called *I'm Telling On You Doug*. These are memories of when I was five years old. This next paragraph is an excerpt from that story describing the abuse that was suffered by myself and my mother, but most importantly, the eventual forgiveness of the whole time.

Down came his hand with a slap, then up flew the fist with a punch and a smothered sound that accompanies the impact of the blow. The rage in his voice mingled with the choreography of two people entangled in a blur of each other's movements. Blood stains are creating new patterns on the dress that my mother is wearing and smearing the floor in the area of this dance of violence. I am paralyzed with fear and apprehension because as I see the blood flowing from my mother's beaten face I can no longer look up at the longing expression of helplessness in her eyes. I feel incapacitated because I am not able to help deliver her from this present anguish. I am slipping into myself as my eyes cannot look beyond the bloodstained waistline of her dress, because beyond this point I cannot understand or carry this hideous image in my psyche. The fabrics of our lives are knitted with screaming, arguing, bludgeon backhands, and the acrimonious intent of our destruction. Will this ever end?

This is a small part of a large story that we suffered until I was five years old. I give testimony that my mother and I are healed and living a blessed life. My mother was restored in her heart and lives a Godly life full of grace for others, while she walks in God's love and in the peace of the power of forgiveness. Matt. 5:44 **But I say unto you, Love your enemies, bless them that curse you, do good to them that hate you, and pray for them which despitefully use you, and persecute you**. Forgiving the unforgivable is what Christ did for each one of us. His grace was extended to me so that I could extend it to my father who truly needed all of our Lord's grace and forgiveness. When you forgive the unforgivable you are allowing all the bondages and family curses to be broken and repeated no more. My family has never felt an angry backhand against their faces. I sow peace into the next generation by forgiving my past. It is time to man up and get healed. Stand tall, put your shoulders back and shout out loud, "I forgive you completely in Christ." Luke 23:34a **Then** said Jesus, Father, forgive them; for they know not what they do.

W.K. Hope said, "Self-discipline is when your conscience tells you to do something and you don't talk back."

Part Seven
Discipline In Finances

There is much to be said on the topic of finances, and the millions of books that have been written on the subject are a testament to the fact that people are looking for answers to creating wealth and security in their lives. The world has sold a bill of goods to the growing population that promotes taking advantage of credit, and being in debt is the normal way to live. Well, the Word of God says it plainly, those who borrow through instruments of debt are servants to the lender, and there is no real freedom until the debt is paid back in full. Prov. 22:7 **The rich rule over the poor, and the borrower is slave to the lender**. Becoming disciplined with our money is a skill that can be practiced, but it takes willpower not to become part of the cycle of spending monies we do not have and on stuff we do not need. The main key that is often missed is that we need to understand finances from God's point of view. God knows there is no lack in the universe and that He has set blessings before us and for us. On the other hand, the enemy of our soul would have us believe that there are shortages in every part of life and we need to take care of number one or someone else will get our share.

The discipline we need to develop is training our hearts and minds to the principles that are in the Word of God. The Lord is a giver and has given us all that is needed to sustain life on this earth and has given us through the sacrifice of His Son Jesus all that will ever be needed to live our lives with the Lord throughout eternity. The lesson God has demonstrated to us is that giving is a way of life and a way to be a hand extended in this world to those who are in need. Luke 6:38 **Give, and it will be given to you. A good measure, pressed down, shaken together, and running over will be poured into your lap. For with the measure you use, it will be measured back to you**.

Being faithful with the finances God allows to flow through our lives is for some, a natural part of their Christian walk, but for others, it is one of the hardest gut-wrenching fights of their faith. The idea of giving some of their hard-earned money to any situation cuts across the grain of their soul. Even though it is the Lord who is prospering them they have no discipline in generosity with their finances. Deut. 8:18 **You shall remember the LORD your God, for it is he who gives you power to get wealth, that he may confirm his covenant that he swore to your fathers, as it is this day**.

There are arguments ad nauseam about giving, tithing, and offerings that support the church assemblies that people attend every Sunday. I do not bother putting my energies into arguing but rather, I discipline my heart to tithe regularly and give when the Holy Spirit prompts my heart to meet a need in a person's life. One of the reasons I remain in this discipline is that I can get out of God's way while He rebukes the devourer for me. Why not allow God to fight my battle for me? I am certain that the Lord can do a much better job of keeping the devil away from destroying my life than I can. Mal. 3:11 **I will rebuke the devourer for you, so that it will not destroy the fruits of your soil, and your vine in the field shall not fail to bear, says the LORD of hosts.**

Our hearts' giving and generosity will demonstrate whether it is genuine or not. How well hidden are the idols we deem more precious than Christ? If our finances are more precious than God, then this trait of heart will reveal itself in no time. Most of the time it is the fear of losing provisions that make some people tighten their grip on what God has given them. If we cannot give ten percent of the amounts we acquire through the labours of life, then we will not be able to hand over the hidden idols lurking in the obscure regions of our souls. If we cannot give of our resources when times are good, how will we rise to full capitulation in Christ when times are difficult in the world? God will eventually ask us to mature in the faith. How can we hear the hard saying of the Lord when we cannot submit to the easier requests of our God? We will stagnate from the idolatry in our hearts and the battle will become much more arduous than needed. I try to remain disciplined in God's basic instruction of finances that go through my hands so that I can hear the Lord when He wants to bless me or use me as His hand extended in the kingdom of our God.

Other Thoughts

Proverbs 22:1 A good name is rather to be chosen than great riches, and

loving favor rather than silver and gold.

When I was a young man I had ten credit cards and, of course, I had ten invoices coming in the mail all the time. The reason was simple, I was only paying the minimum payment on some of the bills. I did not know the Lord personally in those days, but the Spiritual principles and laws of money, wealth, and commerce were at work whether I believed or not. I was guilty of breaking this law. Prov. 3:27 **Withhold not good from them to whom it is due, when it is in the power of thine hand to do it.** I was doing this very thing. I was using the money that belonged to my creditors to self-indulge, therefore, abusing my good name. I was paying less than the minimum payments because I was spending the rest on parties and that lifestyle. There came the day when it all caught up with me and I had to get a bill payer loan. The bank manager cut up all ten credit cards and took care of all the phone calls to the charge card companies to pay the total balances owed. It took me four and a half years at $302.00 a month to pay it all off. In the early 1970's that was a lot of money. During those five years, I used cash only and never again owed anyone an outstanding debt. If I could not pay cash for it, I would not buy it, no matter what "IT" was. Prov. 22:7 **The rich rules over the poor, and the borrower is servant to the lender**. Thank God in the same summer of the final payment paid, I received Christ as my Lord and Savior. Under God's financial principles for living, I have learned how to manage my fiscal affairs. I am often stunned at the financial traps and schemes some Christian brothers find themselves caught up in.

A sister in the Lord that I was counselling for her debt problems had owed a doctor $425.00 for over three years and had not made a payment during that time. She was constantly asking the doctor for more time with his invoice and yet she was traveling to all types of Christian conferences. When we looked into all her debt, there were more creditors owed, and she was testing them the same way. I explained Prov. 3:27 **Withhold not good from them to whom it is due, when it is in the power of thine hand to do it**. The irony would have been funny, but this was pathetic. She was stealing the money owed to the doctor to enhance her Spiritual life in Christ by spending the owed money on Christian conferences. She was not choosing the advice of this Bible verse: Prov. 22:1 **A good name is rather to be chosen than great riches**. She could not understand why she found it so hard to hear God's direction in her life. Mark 4:25 **For he that hath, to him shall be given: and he that hath not, from him shall be taken even that which he hath**. I explained that until she started to seriously deal with her creditors she would find it hard to move forward in the blessing of God's provision. It took a year and a half for her to pay off her outstanding debts, but finally came to a place where Rom. 13:8a **Owe no man any thing, but to love one another**, had become real to her.

I was parked in front of a large drugstore, and I noticed a sign in their window that said "SALE ON STUFF." I realized that we have become so conditioned to buying on impulse, that the sign said it all. We, as a nation, are going into extreme debt over stuff and more stuff. The hole in our hearts cannot be filled with stuff. It can only be filled with Christ Himself. Gal. 2:20 **I am crucified with Christ: nevertheless I live; yet not I, but Christ lives in me: and the life which I now live in the flesh I live by the faith of the Son of God,**

who loved me and gave Himself for me. The principle of God's financial grace will come to you when you seek Him first and ask Him for help in becoming disciplined in your financial responsibilities. Matt. 6:33 **But seek ye first the kingdom of God, and his righteousness; and all these things shall be added unto you**.

Part Eight
Discipline In Relationship And Friendship

Relationships would be easy to deal with if there were no people involved. Relationships would be fine and smooth going if everyone agreed with me. Well, the facts are that relationships can and are sometimes messy. I think the discipline needed in relationships will mainly depend on our ability to be a gracious person because eventually friendships and relationships will be tested. One of the more difficult areas of friendship is knowing when it is time to cut off or get away from a toxic relationship. There are always conflicting feelings being fueled by the edicts of Christianity fighting for primacy in the back of our conscience. We know that we are not healthy being around these people and we need to get away from them, but the swirling thoughts and questions come along and accuse our hearts of not being like our Lord. We ask ourselves things like, "Doesn't God want us to love all people, and wouldn't I be turning my back on this needy person? I can't handle the unbearable pressure this person is using to destroy my life, but maybe God wants to teach me something about suffering. If I leave these people to the sins they are practising and want me to get involved with, will God be angry with me for abandoning them?"

We need to know the difference when we are to keep supporting, helping, and giving of our time to those who are rejecting God's council and knowing when it is time to redirect our ministerial hearts toward others whom God has placed in our path to be saved, healed, and redeemed. Prov. 1:10 **My child, if sinners entice you, turn your back on them!** We will need to learn how to make these crucial choices with the discernment of the Holy Spirit who will lead us to fulfil the work in God's kingdom. Once a toxic person is argumentative and is continually rejecting every thought and idea that you bring to help them gain victory, then it is time to do as Timothy says, 2Tim. 2:23 **Don't have anything to do with foolish and stupid arguments, because you know they produce quarrels**. Once quarrels become the norm then we need to move on to those who are hungry for a righteous life. There is a proviso to think about. David Kalamen says it this way, "Though we may never "cut off" people as we are redemptive in heart, we must realize that people cut themselves off and we need to recognize God-established boundaries, so we are not compromised by our association." I agree with what David is saying. Therefore, I will try to remain open to those who have cut themselves off, if and when they repent and return to following

Christ Jesus. No one is without hope when
the rebellion of the heart is finally repented
of.

Now on the other hand, when you have
poured your heart and time into people who
are walking in the truth of God's Word that
they have gleaned through all the lessons
learned and are growing in the power of
the Holy Spirit, then keep growing with
them until God directs them into what He
is calling them to do. Be disciplined of heart
and mind when you see God transferring
a person you have sown your life into
being sent on an assignment from God.
Do not worry about losing the friendship
that was developed because no matter the
time apart there will be a God-living root
of grace connecting both your hearts until
the end. Prov. 18:14b **But there is a friend
who sticks closer than a brother**. The
purpose of discipleship/relationship in
Christ is to help righteous people become
great advocates for the Lord's kingdom and
make disciples who will be holy salt for the
souls of men who are lost in this world.

This is not a law nor a fundamental

belief, but only my thoughts on the matter. Becoming disciplined in relationships and friendships will help us keep our souls from the heartbreak and painful disappointment of those who have fallen along the way. Thank God there is redemption for these people if they accept the grace offered and repent. However, nothing hurts so much as to have walked with a brother or sister through the hard times battling for God's kingdom, to find out that they had nuked their lives through sin. No matter what the sin is, the disappointment is palpable within our hearts (it seems this way for me), and we must hand these feelings that can crush our souls over to the Lord. We need to find grace for ourselves in these moments of spiritual anguish as well as have grace for those we now feel compelled to pray for in earnest. Even if the fallen are avoiding your calls because of the shame they are going through, we need God's discipline of heart to keep our lives in front of God's face so that we may be available to snatch them from the clutches of the enemy. Jude 1:23 **Save others, snatching them out of the**

fire; and on some have mercy with fear, hating even the garment polluted by the flesh. No one said this life journey of faith in Christ would be easy, but with the Lord watching our backs, through the discipline God has instilled within our souls, this too can be conquered. To be disciplined in relationships, friendships, and discipleship is a weapon we need to become skilled at. Only the blood of Jesus can keep us all together in the love and relationship we have with our Heavenly Father. Nothing else matters but that God is honoured with our lives, as we live for His pleasure.

Other Thoughts

Rodney King: "I just want to say, you know, can we all get along?"

It will be very difficult for all to get along because it takes discipline to do so. I was reading in the Gospel of Luke where the disciples were arguing as to who was greater. Luke 9:46 **An argument started** among the disciples as to which of them would be the greatest. Gal. 5: 26 **Let us not be desirous of vain glory, provoking one another, envying one another**. The thought struck me that even in the company of Jesus it still took discipline to control their volatile emotions and it took willpower to overcome the temptations of power and control.

We are, after all, created in the image of God and were given dominion on the earth. So the desire to take control and create something from our hearts comes honestly. The problem, of course, came with the fall of man and man's desire was corrupted to the point of even wanting God under our feet. Isa. 14:12 **How art thou fallen from heaven, O Lucifer, son of the morning! how art thou cut down to the ground, which didst weaken the nations!** 13 **For thou hast said in thine heart, I will ascend into heaven, I will exalt my throne above the stars of God: I will sit also upon the mount of the congregation, in the sides of the north:** 14 **I will ascend above the heights of the clouds; I will be like the**

most High. Because of our fallen nature that was corrupted by this narcissistic sinful angel Lucifer, we now need to be disciplined by God to walk in the power of the Holy Spirit. The good news is that we have been given the grace to walk out our Christian lives as we learn to be disciples of Christ. It is as if we were granted the privilege and blessing to learn how to play the violin in public with none of the harsh criticisms and vitriolic shouts to shut up!

We were saved and we are being saved and we will be saved because of this grace that we are covered in. The discipline or rod of correction over our lives is not irksome or harsh. It is the blessing of the Lord that corrects us. Prov. 3:12 **For the LORD disciplines the one He loves, just as a father, the son he delights in**. Some of us might have a negative connotation as to the meaning of the word discipline. Many think of childhood beatings that left unresolved anger and lifelong scars. That is not what God does. The reader's digest version for the word discipline is: *In its natural sense, discipline is systematic instruction* *intended to train a person, sometimes literally called a disciple, in a craft, trade or other activity, or to follow a particular code of conduct.* We are all being disciplined to be who God created us to be and the Lord does everything out of love.

His guidance in our lives will also be motivated the same way—out of love. Why would God use love to discipline us? 1John 4:18 **There is no fear in love; but perfect love casts out fear: because fear hath torment. He that fears is not made perfect in love**. This is why we can trust the discipline of the Lord because it will eventually produce love. Will the discipline always feel good? No! However, the fruit and results will be glorious and eternal. I have shared this before but it is worth repeating. I was angry at myself one day because I had sinned. I heard the Spirit of God ask me, "Are you angry because you vexed the Holy Spirit, or are you angry because you broke your personal righteousness record?" It was clear that I did not care about vexing the Holy Spirit because the question would not have been asked. It looked like I was in for some correction with the rod of

God's love. Was I embarrassed, ashamed and feeling a bit uncertain? Yup! All three feelings were screaming in my head, but God loved me through it by reaching my heart. I repented and peace came just as our loving Father said it would. Phil. 4:7 **And the peace of God, which passes all understanding, shall keep your hearts and minds through Christ Jesus**.

Don't be afraid of the correction and discipline that comes from our Lord. It is life to our very being and the very foundation of relationship with God and one another. The key to keeping our relationships clean and forthright is remaining disciplined in our hearts to not be offended by our friends, peers, and neighbours when either of us fall short in life. We will need to learn how to listen to one another and be willing to give God's blessings to those we don't always agree with. We need to choose to get along. 1Cor. 9:20 **And to the Jews I became like a Jew, so that I might win the Jews. To those under the Law, as under the Law (myself not being under the Law) so that I might win those under the Law**.

Other Thoughts

Proverbs 27:6 Wounds from a sincere friend are better than many kisses from an enemy.

Some of the greatest dysfunctional crashes that show up in people's lives are when a family secret is found out, or it has been unintentionally exposed. This can happen through a misspoken word, or when an innocent, or not so innocent statement is blurted out. "Oh, I thought you knew you were adopted. I thought it was common knowledge that your father had been in prison for embezzlement. Your mother died in an insane asylum, not a general hospital. Didn't your father tell you that mental illness was a problem in the family?" Many have heard worse things and it changed their lives and family relationships forever.

Most parents tell their children to

always tell the truth. The children grow up to find out that they had been lied to their whole lives, because of a family secret that was covered up and deemed embarrassing or shameful. Psalm 44:21 **Shall not God search this out? for he knoweth the secrets of the heart**. At that point, how do these parents ask their children to trust them? Their argument for the family deception is often, "I just wanted to protect the children's hearts from getting hurt. Can't they see that? We were trying to do the right thing." Prov. 27:6 **Wounds from a sincere friend are better than many kisses from an enemy**. How does the family member who fostered the secret ask the other members of the family not to react in shame, mistrust, embarrassment, or deep-seated guilt? How do they heal the rift that is now showing up in the once-amiable relationship? Depending on the weight and seriousness of the secret, the response can be devastating. The reaction within the heart of the one who was kept in the dark can be far more grievous than what was being covered up in the first place.

My father found out in his early twenties that his last name he had used throughout his life, was not the name on his new and real birth certificate he had applied for. To join the army, my father needed proper documentation. That was when he found out there had been a family secret. The anger that arose in him because of this secret caused him to hate and mistrust family members from that time on. Psalm 64:2 **Hide me from the secret plots of the wicked, from the throng of evildoers**. I don't know all the reasons why my father became the angry, abusive, and peevish person he was. He had many abnormal problems going on in his mind and soul. He was a broken man who hit first and justified his cowardice behaviour with raging expletives. I think the family secret he stumbled upon was, in his mind, a betrayal that led him farther away from family and eventually all friendships. John Lennon said, "One thing you can't hide – is when you're crippled inside."

Joseph's brothers had a terrible family secret. They lived with a very dark deception they had all taken part in. They deceived their father, Jacob, into believing Joseph had been killed by a wild beast. Gen. 37:31 **So they took Joseph's robe, slaughtered a male goat, and dipped the robe in its blood. 32 They sent the robe of many colors to their father and said, "We found this. Examine it. Is it your son's robe or not?"** In fact, the brothers had sold Joseph into slavery. This secret had gnawed at them for about twenty-seven years before it had finally been exposed in full. Num. 32:23b **Be sure your sin will catch up with you**. What an emotional mess this secret caused in all the family member's lives.

I have noticed that young people today have heard everything there is when it comes to family dysfunction and outright freakiness. Many young people's classmates and contemporaries have all grown up with multiple parenting arrangements and dysfunction on a daily basis. It has not made them secure people, but they have seen and heard way more than what is being hidden in some families. Letting them know the facts of what happened during their family life–whether horrific or embarrassing–can be emotionally carried when it is honestly and gently brought out into the open. The problem arises when things are found out by accident, or someone stumbles across paperwork that tells them a different story than the one they grew up with. That stings more than the secret itself. Being babied, overparented, and mollycoddled can seem like they were seen as mentally unfit and did not have the emotional capability to handle family matters. That is what hurts, and brings out hateful reactions, plus the cycle of secrecy may just become the way to handle things for the next generation. We often become what we hate.

Read the Bible and you will notice that family history is clearly exposed. There are murderers, prostitutes, adulterers, and many other sin-drenched people in Jesus' lineage. God does not hide any of it from us. Psalm 90:8 **You have set our iniquities before you, our secret sins in the light of your presence**. It is all exposed because exposed secrets have no power over you. When sin, deceptions, and secrets are known, no one has power over you or can threaten you by divulging the secret because it is a secret no more. I am not advocating that you plaster every terrible secret on a social media platform for all to read. Keep the family mess in the house, then clean the house. Don't create more hurts than there are already. Try not to be indignant or offended by what is said. Keep the conversation respectful and react with a willingness to forgive, because everyone involved needs healing. Nothing remains a secret in the family forever, so become disciplined in repairing the split that has happened to family members because of hidden secrets. Mark 4:22 **For there is nothing hidden which will not be revealed, nor has anything been kept secret but that it should come to light**. Through prayer, if you ask God, He will give you the courage to heal the wounds in your family relationships.

Jim Rohn said, "For every disciplined effort, there is a multiple reward."

Part Nine
Discipline In Suffering

Suffering is not a popular topic in some church circles. For some reason, this subject seems to depict "less than," or "not as spiritual" as those who have conquered all manner of suffering. The constant teaching that *you can have anything you want from God if you believe*, has made it difficult for those who are suffering through sickness, poverty, and emptiness of soul. Those who are suffering feel twice as pained because they can't break through to the advertised victory side of living that seems so easy to get to according to some ministries. There is a difference between having a positive outlook in our faith because we truly know in our hearts that nothing is impossible for God, and the manipulative chanting of certain verses we think will deliver us from our present lot in life. Yes, go ahead and proclaim the promises of God and stand firm on the anointed Word of God but know that breakthrough sometimes comes at a cost to our flesh and soul.

The Apostle Paul was acquainted with suffering on many levels. Paul was not ashamed or reluctant to talk about his suffering. The thing he did not do was complain about it. 2Cor. 11:23 **Are they servants of Christ? I'm talking like a madman — I'm a better one: with far more labors, many more imprisonments, far worse beatings, many times near death. 24 Five times I received the forty lashes minus one from the Jews. 25 Three times I was beaten with rods. Once I received a stoning. Three times I was shipwrecked. I have spent a night and a day in the open sea. 26 On frequent journeys, I faced dangers from rivers, dangers from robbers, dangers from my own people, dangers from Gentiles, dangers in the city, dangers in the wilderness, dangers at sea, and** dangers among false brothers; 27 **toil and hardship, many sleepless nights, hunger and thirst, often without food, cold, and without clothing**. Paul is pointing out that he had learned through suffering that he could have victory in his walk with the Lord.

I do not know how you can read the above scriptures and pretend that suffering will not be something we will go through. Was the Apostle Paul at the beginning of a new dispensation and were the times under Roman occupation harsh? Yes, but so are the poor saints who live in North Korea, Syria, Venezuela, Russia and many other places where the persecution of Christians is a normal event. The discipline it takes to rise above the suffering and remain grateful to our Lord amid the suffering is an acquired skill of understanding that no matter what we are going through, we are truly and continually loved by God.

The Lord of Glory went to the cross and took the suffering that was the result of sin with Him and that suffering was nailed to the cross during Jesus' time of torment and separation from His Heavenly Father. Jesus walked as a man and was tempted in all areas as we are but suffered through the temptations of life. Heb. 5:8 **Even though Jesus was God's Son, he learned obedience from the things he suffered**. Our discipline in suffering is to make us better and give us the vision for a victorious future and the ability to help those who are suffering the shame, regrets, and disappointments of a life gone by. If the suffering of these souls is because of sin we can help them become washed in the cleansing blood of the Lord. If their suffering is because they have chosen Christ as Lord we can uphold them in prayer and lift them up to try again. Prov. 24:16a **For a righteous person falls seven times and rises again**. If the righteous man has fallen seven times and got back up, there has been a certain amount of suffering that went along with that fight to get back up. Through suffering, they created a discipline in their relationship with Christ that causes strength from within and from above to take hold of that righteous man's heart, and that is what I call victory.

My pastor, David Kalamen and I have had conversations about suffering to determine how we are to go through this hard part of our walk in Christ. I wanted his thoughts on the subject because I know that he has suffered from major health problems that have threatened his life. He has suffered heartbreaking betrayal in ministry, and has suffered loss in business. I can say he is a man acquainted with suffering and pain. Pastor David's response to some of the things we talked about is as written, "If we are afraid of the pain of crucifixion, we will never know the joy of resurrection life. Suffering is a form of dying to self that becomes like a seed germinating in the ground of God. You never know what it will produce. I have found that my response to suffering has been four-fold: if there is any sense of missing the mark, I repent; if there is a sense of spiritual battle, I resist; if there is understanding, I rejoice; if there is no understanding, I relent and wait for God to make things clear."

What I see in David's explanation with

his four chosen responses to the suffering he is going through, seems to say that it takes discipline of heart and will to remain faithful towards the heart of God and to call on Him for deliverance consistently during our times of suffering. We do not ignore the suffering but like everything else in our walk with the Lord we bring our requests and questions to God our Father by faith. The thing is, where are we going to go if not to God? As the Apostle Peter so profoundly said when asked by Jesus If he would also leave because of the hard doctrines being taught, we too need to answer the same question. What else can we say when going through suffering but, "Lord, to whom will we go, You have the words of life that we need at this moment." John 6:68 **Simon Peter answered Him, "Lord, to whom shall we go? You have the words of eternal life**.

It is difficult to remain disciplined in trusting God when pain is screaming, throbbing, and dictating the choices we need to make through a painful day. It is easy to shut down and want to give up on life because, in the back of our minds, many souls are saying, "This is not abundant life, this is too hard to bear!" I agree that pain can make us reach for every kind of relief out there, from snake oil cures to addictive prescription drugs—just give me something for the pain!!! I have not reached the spiritual maturity that Paul exhibits when he encourages the persecuted believers in Christ to go on in the faith regardless of the suffering they are going through. The Apostle Paul calls all the pain, persecution, and trials of our life -these momentary light afflictions. 2Cor. 4:17 **For our momentary light affliction is producing for us an absolutely incomparable eternal weight of glory**. The only answer I have for my present state of maturity in my walk with Christ is to say, "I know, my Redeemer lives." This is the thought that keeps me reaching toward the next step in disciplining my heart when I am suffering. Keep believing and trusting in the sovereignty of our Lord Jesus Christ. He is the author and finisher of our faith, and that is where we need to bring our hearts. As difficult as it may seem to do, we need to embrace what James says, "Count it all joy, brethren." James 1:2 **Consider it a great joy, my brothers and sisters, whenever you experience various trials, 3 because you know that the testing of your faith produces endurance.**

As long as we are on this side of eternity, suffering will be a challenge in our lives. I do not believe that we need to be plowed under by all the suffering. There is hope in the delivering Word of the Lord. What I do know is that I need to stay disciplined in the faith that God has given me through His Son Jesus, so that my strength is renewed daily and able to fight the good fight of faith that we have all been called to take part in. May God's eternal grace cover our shortcomings and lift us into His presence so that we may honour Him with our lives. I hope that it may be said of me, that I was tested and approved in Christ.

Other Thoughts

A lot of people talk a big talk until they are going through a time of suffering. If ever there was a time to double down on being disciplined, it is during our times of suffering. We do not suffer well and find it hard to see the need for it even when the Word of God says to take the suffering as a growing opportunity. James 1:2 **Dear brothers and sisters, when troubles come your way, consider it an opportunity for great joy.** 3 **For you know that when your faith is tested, your endurance has a chance to grow**. What an inconvenient Scripture this is for this self-gratifying society who considered great suffering to be the electrical power going out for a few hours, or our flight being delayed because of technical issues.

When our children reject us, the suffering is palpable and the deep wounding taking place in our hearts makes it hard to believe that God loves our children more than we do. What? How can God love my child more than I do? The question remains, "How can God understand the pain we are going through?" Maybe your spouse has betrayed you and the pain feels like it has entered the deepest part of your soul and your bones are throbbing in anguish every waking moment and the only relief comes when you sleep just to escape the suffering.

Where does the strength of our discipline come from in that time of need? Why does it hurt so much when your spouse says, "You are a loser," or you are acting like a crazy person? Why does it hurt the deepest parts within us when something your spouse uses against you that was first revealed in a time of vulnerable confession and intimacy, but is now being thrust forth as a weapon to humiliate and degrade your existence?

This type of hurt happens when you start to believe the words of malice being used against you. Once you believe the words being used against you, the discipline needed in your soul to fight back to the reality of truth can be a battle of battles.

This is why becoming disciplined in suffering is important. A disciplined mind learns how to look past the hurting words that almost become believable. Know your value. Jesus died for you because He saw the infinite value the Godhead placed on your soul. Therefore, shouldn't we rather believe the words of love that God speaks of us and says to us?

When we are betrayed by parents, family, friends, or church members, and we feel that these people who should know better have disrespected us by the way we became a punching bag or a dumping ground for their inadequacies and cowardice, the suffering can be harder to bear. Psalm 55:12 **For it was not an enemy that reproached me; Then I could have borne it: Neither was it he that hated me that did magnify himself against me; Then I would have hid myself from him:** 13 **But it is you, a man like myself, my companion and close friend.** Discipline in the area of suffering is an acquired skill that can only be righteously developed in the resurrection power of the cross, and the atoning blood of our Lord Jesus. We need to pick up our cross and follow Jesus to the place of reconciliation with all men. Whether it is family, friends, or neighbours who have harmed us, we are not diminished by the suffering they have caused, but rather through Christ we are resurrected to honest victory and restoration of heart.

Part Ten
Discipline In Thankfulness, Gratitude, and Attitude

The act of being thankful for everything is what God asks us to do. It takes habitual discipline to remain grateful for the blessings in our lives. We need to practice the art of expressing gratitude within our hearts and be consistent in extending thanks in all manner of situations including the difficult ones. 1Thes. 5:18 **Give thanks in everything, for this is the will of God**

toward you in Christ Jesus. The question we need to answer is—why is it so hard to say "Thank you" and remain grateful throughout our lives? Why are we so easily dissatisfied and quick to complain that we have nothing, when in fact, at this time in history, we have more than anyone has ever owned, possessed and acquired? I believe the short answer is that God is asking us to give thanks in all things, and this command alone means the enemy of our soul is going to go out of his way to make sure we are never satisfied, grateful, or thankful for anything. Even though the Word tells us that all good gifts come from God, Satan will point out every flaw in everything we have, and everything we are doing just to get us complaining so that ungratefulness starts to slip into our hearts.

There is an all-out battle against our souls in this area of life because the enemy knows the moment we become a thankful and grateful people we will have destroyed the works of the enemy and will have caused great damage to the kingdom of darkness. Murmuring and ungratefulness were the weapons the enemy provoked in the children of Israel that brought about the judgment of the Lord. After the arduous journey and time in the wilderness, the Lord sent twelve spies to scope out the land of Canaan that God had promised to give the children of Israel. Ten of the spies reported that everything in the land was as God said, full of milk and honey, or as would be said today—a dream property. However, the focus of the ten spies were on the people who were living there and they were fearful of the people and saw themselves as grasshoppers or insignificant in their sight. The evil report as it is known, caused an immediate depression among the people and they even said things to the effect that they had been better off dead. Have you ever responded to God in this manner? Num.14:2 **And all the children of Israel complained against Moses and Aaron, and the whole congregation said to them, "If only we had died in the land of Egypt! Or if only we had died in this wilderness!** The murmuring took root in all the people's hearts and no matter how much

Caleb and Joshua proclaimed the opposite, that they had God on their side and could well take the land, the ungrateful hearts won out and brought about a judgment upon the people. The sad thing was that the nation of Israel was on the doorstep of receiving God's promise but was not able to attain it because of a majority vote from a fickle and undisciplined people who believed the fears of the ten spies. Their choices led to being ungrateful and without gratitude for what God had done for them to that point.

In many cases, people are doing the same thing today. Even though they claim to know God they do not give thanks to Him for their lives or anything in it. Rom. 1:21 **Yes, they knew God, but they wouldn't worship him as God or even give Him thanks. And they began to think up foolish ideas of what God was like. As a result, their minds became dark and confused**. The dissatisfaction of the hour needs to be quelled by a change of heart that may be very radical to some but absolutely needed to get through all the anger that is being screamed out in the world. Ungratefulness produces an angry response to everything going on that seems to take away from one's life. Nothing satisfies and therefore no sense of accomplishment can be achieved because the big empty hole in the soul of the thankless keeps on growing and harder to fill with the stuff of the world. We need to become people who daily express thankfulness. We need to stop and declare how grateful we are for who we are in Christ, and what we have at this time in our lives, because today is the moment we are living in. This is the day the Lord has made for us to come to Him with thanksgiving in our hearts.

If you are waiting until all is right with the world and everything is just perfect in your lives before you start to give thanks to God, then you will never open your mouth in thanksgiving. There will always be something missing in your insatiable wants. The greed that lurks in the dark places of your heart will show up proclaiming injustice and that you are being wronged because you cannot have everything your heart desires. You will replace God who is supposed to be on the throne of your heart with the stuff you do not have yet. You will not have developed a discipline of gratefulness but will have created a lifelong existence of discontent and a soul that is always in need of rescuing from the abyss of emptiness. The only way out of this cycle of ungratefulness is to start voicing out loud all the blessings that are right in front of you. Start with the obvious facts that you can breathe, walk, and talk—start there! Just shout it out—"THANK YOU, LORD!"

Other Thoughts

1Chronicles 16:34 Give thanks to the Lord, for He is good; His love endures forever.

I am in my seventies, and I was reflecting on the events of my God-given life. I am very grateful to God for my good health, sharp mind (if I may say so), and all the blessings I have had in this short life. I can now say like the Psalmist, "I have not seen the seed of the righteous begging bread." Psalm 37:25 **I have been young, and now am old; yet have I not seen the righteous forsaken, nor his seed begging bread**. I have had the pleasure of seeing the truth of this verse take place in my family and other families' lives. Gratitude to God in life is what will help us get through life with the joy of the Lord. When gratitude is part of our character, we will have the favour of God working on our behalf and we will be fulfilling God's will for our life. 1Thes. 5:18 **In every thing give thanks: for this is the will of God in Christ Jesus concerning you.** Simply offering thanks and gratefulness to God in whatever we are going through will turn our captivity around while we are being strengthened in our hearts. Job 42:10 **And the LORD turned the captivity of Job, when he prayed for his friends: also the LORD gave Job twice as much as he had before**.

The reason we move with gratitude toward God in life is that we will help the next generation become grateful followers of Christ. If our children do not see the fruit of our thankfulness and gratefulness taking an authentic place in our hearts and marking our lives with concrete spiritual substance, then why should they follow a rote and insipid existence in the church? If we cannot find ourselves in a place of gratefulness toward Christ for all that He has done for us, why then would our children want a milquetoast relationship with a Saviour not worth thanking? Psalm 107:1 **O give thanks unto the LORD, for He is good: for His mercy endures for ever**.

One of the reasons that God made a covenant with Abraham was that Abraham agreed to teach his children about God. Gen. 18:18a **Seeing that Abraham shall surely become a great and mighty nation,**19 **For I know him, that he will command his children and his household after him, and they shall keep the way of the LORD, to do justice and judgment; that the LORD may bring upon Abraham that which he hath spoken of him**. I am not saying that if your children are not walking with God that you have failed as a Christian parent, or have not exhibited the life of Christ at work in your life. Please do not read that lie of the devil into what I am saying. I am saying that first, we must find the joy of gratitude in our walk with God before we can freely and joyfully express it with love toward others. You know this first-hand to be true. When you are full of gratefulness and thanksgiving, life looks brighter and feels lighter. Even people in the world see it. Friedrich Nietzsche said, "The essence of all beautiful art, all great art, is gratitude." I look back and say, "Thank you, Lord," with gratefulness to all the great men and women of God that have influenced my life toward righteousness. I am full of thankfulness for my wife and her true love for me and who we have become after decades of marriage.

I am grateful that my sons have turned out to be wonderful young men that will be a blessing on this earth. I am so grateful that I have never been unemployed over the last fifty years. I am full of gratitude that my wife and I have no debt whatsoever, and all that we have is paid for. Better still, I am so thankful for the many years of walking with my Lord and Savior Jesus Christ. I am full of gratitude for all the healing, provisions, protections, directions and love that the Lord has lavished on my life. What can I do but give thanks to a wonderful Heavenly Father who gave everything for me? Eph. 5:20 **Giving thanks always for all things unto God and the Father in the name of our Lord Jesus Christ**. I am grateful that I have become thankful and that I can see that the seed of the righteous shall be delivered. I ask God, in Jesus' name, for all our children to be saved and reconciled with Christ, and that we all come to know and accept Jesus as our Lord and Saviour. Amen.

John Maxwell said, "Discipline helps us start. Discipline helps us finish."

In Conclusion
Finish Strong

Jeremiah 12:5 If you have run with the footmen, and they have wearied you, then how can you contend with horses? And if in the land of peace, in which you trusted, they wearied you, then how will you do in the floodplain of the Jordan?

Finish strong, or however you want to say it, "Finish strong, finish hard, or finish right." Do your best to finish the race God has placed you in with the life He has given you. I caught myself looking at the clock at the gym and wondering how much time I had left to complete my workout. I quickly reprimanded myself for looking for an easy finish. I had to say out loud, "Come on Norm, finish strong!" When I catch myself making up excuses for being a slacker in things that need to get done, I often think of Jeremiah's words, "If you have run with the footmen, and they have wearied you, then how can you contend with horses?"

How true is that? If I can't do the things that I need to do daily, what am I going to do if times get really hard? If I can't pray and spend time with God when the days are good, how will I ask for help during a frantic panic of events when the world is crashing around me? If I cannot control my eating habits and make sure I am exercising regularly, how will I find the courage and willpower to work out and eat properly when a diagnosis of multiple deadly conditions comes rushing at me like an armed bandit to take over my existence? How can I finish strong when all my choices are weak and undisciplined wishful thinking? Prov. 14:23 **All hard work brings a profit, but mere talk leads only to poverty**.

We hear people say these wishful things all the time. I wish I could get up early and spend time with the Lord. I wish I could get to work on time. I wish I could push away from the table when I am full. Prov. 13:4 **A sluggard's appetite is never filled, but the desires of the diligent are fully satisfied**. I wish I would get off my lazy butt and do what needs to be done. On and on the wishing goes. To be able to finish strong, we need to become strong in the areas of life where God has sown inspirational tenacity within us to accomplish what we were created to fulfill. Prov. 23:7a **For as he thinks within himself, so he is**. We need to break through the walls of laziness that everyone has experienced throughout their lives. Not everyone is hard-wired to take on every challenge that comes their way. Some will need to apply much more effort than others just to accomplish small tasks. That is fine, as long as you finish strong and go on to the next Godly life-changing lesson for living in Christ's righteousness.

For some, making their bed before they leave home may be the Goliath they need to conquer, and for others, it may be finishing their doctorate in the field of learning that burns in their hearts. Nevertheless, whatever magnitude the task is, finishing strong will help determine the character of heart one has in life. I was asked, what if I had a very short time to live, and the book I was writing would not get finished? I said, "I reckon I would write faster." Not trying to be a wise guy, but these hypothetical questions of "what if" do not matter when you are living your best life to the fullest and are doing the best you can with what the Lord has given you. Besides, it is God who determines what we do and eventually accomplish. Yes, we are willing participants in the plan God has for us, therefore, worrying about what gets finished in our lives is His problem. I say this reverently because God has the number of our days in His hands. Our job or raison d'etre is to go forth in Christ's righteousness and finish the race set before us.

I am sure the Apostle Paul could have done much more had he not been killed during Nero's reign of persecution towards the Christians. He knew his time was short. Paul declares that he will finish strong and that there will be a blessed reward at the end of it all. 2Tim. 4:6 **For I am already being poured out like a drink offering, and the time for my departure is near.** 7 **I have fought the good fight, I have finished the race, I have kept the faith.** He finished his race even though he had the knowledge and capacity to have done much more. My point is that Paul finished strong, and we are blessed because of it. We have his letters to the church which help, direct, and instruct us to live in Christ's righteousness.

Whatever the trials and tribulations that show up on our road to eternity are, they can be conquered with the help and guidance of the Holy Spirit. The thing that is often missing in Christians' lives is the will within a person to move ahead when the Spirit of God is prodding them along. Many become weary and tired because they do not do the small things their faith requires to grow. Complacency becomes a default setting in the heart, and insipidness becomes the fruit of their day-to-day existence. The Word expressly warns us not to give up on what God has inspired us to sow into. Gal. 6:9 **And let us not grow weary of doing good, for in due season we will reap, if we do not give up**. If God has given us a vision, then God will give us the means to fulfill it and finish strong. How good is that?

Note To Self

As I wrote at the beginning of this book, I have not reached the perfection of discipline nor have I attained all its attributes, but have endeavoured to become a better version of myself through the finished work of the cross and my Lord Jesus. Jesus is the author and finisher of my faith and life. Therefore, I live to honour Him and will keep trying to do so until I stand in joy before Him on that great and glorious day. Blessing to all who walk that journey with me.

About The Author

I have been in Christian ministry in one form or another for over forty years. In 1980 I attended Commonwealth Bible College in Katoomba, New South Wales, Australia. At that time I was involved in prison ministries, preaching on the radio in a small town, and church-related works of all kinds. I have taught bible college courses and also have been involved in personal discipleship training. God has blessed me all along the way. Now I have the opportunity to write down what was experienced throughout the years. The Lord has blessed me with sound and forthright material to write a series of Christian devotionals. I have lived the testimonies on these pages and can attest to the fact that God is so faithful and good. My hope is that your soul will be enriched as you read this book. God bless you.

Connect With Norm

Norm's Blog can now be found online in
English, French and Spanish.
Your comments on any of the hundreds of
blog posts are appreciated.
English sirnorm.com
French sirnorm.com/fr/
Spanish sirnorm.com/es/

www.ingramcontent.com/pod-product-compliance
Lightning Source LLC
La Vergne TN
LVHW051521080426
835509LV00017B/2147
* 9 7 8 1 9 8 8 2 2 6 6 6 8 *